S0-BBF-017

PORTRAITS
IN PRINT

PORTRAITS IN PRINT

■

A COLLECTION OF PROFILES AND THE STORIES BEHIND THEM

■

HELEN BENEDICT

Afterword by Jessica Mitford

COLUMBIA UNIVERSITY PRESS • NEW YORK

Columbia University Press
New York Oxford
Copyright © 1991 Helen Benedict
All rights reserved

Library of Congress Cataloging-in-Publication Data
Benedict, Helen.
Portraits in print : a collection of profiles and the stories
behind them / Helen Benedict : afterword by Jessica Mitford.
p.   cm.
Includes bibliographical references and index.
Contents: The passionate mind, Susan Sontag—Flight from
predictability, Joseph Brodsky—Undaunted and undefeated, Beverly
Sills—Filling silences with strong voices, Paule Marshall—
Morals and surprises, Bernard Malamud—Intrepid twosome, Jessica
Mitford and Robert Treuhaft—A talk with Leonard Michaels—A day
in the life of an unknown poet, Bertrand Bard—Never insult a
Yiddish typewriter, Isaac Bashevis Singer.
ISBN 0-231-07226-0
1. Celebrities—United States—Biography.   2. Authors,
American—20th century—Biography.   3. Biography (as a literary
form) I. Title.
CT220.B45 1991
920.073—dc20   90–41700   CIP

Casebound editions of Columbia University Press books are Smyth-sewn
and printed on permanent and durable acid-free paper

∞

Printed in the United States of America
c 10 9 8 7 6 5 4 3 2 1

To Marion and Burton Benedict,
who gave me the first tools

CONTENTS

CONTENTS

ACKNOWLEDGMENTS

My thanks go to Bernard Taper for teaching me what a profile is; to Jennifer Crewe for believing and encouraging, and, most of all, to the nine interviewees in this book, who gave me the time, patience, and liberty to probe into their lives.

I wish to thank the following publications for permission to reprint the articles collected in this book:

"The Passionate Mind," by Helen Benedict first appeared in *New York Woman* in November 1988.

"Flight from Predictability: Joseph Brodsky" by Helen Benedict first appeared in the *Antioch Review* (February 1985), vol. 43, no. 1. Copyright © 1985 by the Antioch Review, Inc.

"Undaunted and Undefeated: Beverly Sills" and "Filling Silences with Strong Voices: Paule Marshall" by Helen Benedict are reprinted with the permission of the New York City Commission on the Status of Women, and first appeared in *Women Making History: Conversations With Fifteen New Yorkers*, 1985, edited by Maxine Gold.

"Bernard Malamud: Morals and Surprises" by Helen Benedict first appeared in the *Antioch Review* (February 1983), vol. 41, no. 1. Copyright © 1983 by the Antioch Review, Inc.

"Intrepid Twosome" by Helen Benedict first appeared in the *Berkeley Monthly*, March 1981.

"A Talk With Leonard Michaels" by Helen Benedict first appeared in the *New York Times Book Review*, April 12, 1981. Copyright © by the New York Times Company. Reprinted by permission.

"A Day in the Life of an Unknown Poet" originally appeared under the title "Bombing Benignly in Berkeley" in *California Living*, the magazine of the *San Francisco Sunday Examiner and Chronicle*, July 23, 1978, p. 22; © 1978 San Francisco Examiner. Reprinted by permission.

Material from "Never Insult a Yiddish Typewriter" excerpted from "Never Insult a Yiddish Typewriter, and Other Gentle Wisdom from Isaac Bashevis Singer" by Helen Benedict, which first appeared in *Writer's Digest*, May 1980; from "Conversations with Isaac Singer" by Helen Benedict, which first appeared in *California Living*, November 11, 1979; from "Demons, Goblins, and Autobiography: An Interview with Isaac Bashevis Singer" by Helen Benedict, which first appeared in the *San Francisco Review of Books*, vol. 4, no. 3; and from "Singer the Storyteller" by Helen Benedict, which first appeared in *New Wings*, 1979.

PREFACE

Objective biography is logically and artistically impossible. "Observation is always selective" as Karl Popper reminds us. Every observation, he explains, requires "a chosen object, a definite task, an interest, a point of view, a problem" otherwise it is valueless.

—IRA BRUCE NADEL,
Biography: Fiction, Fact, and Form[1]

■

E very piece of journalism has a secret history: how the reporter thought of the idea, what the interviewer was really trying to find out, how the writer arranged the piece, what the reporter really thought of the subject, what went on behind the scenes and never reached print. As objective as a reporter tries to be, this secret history is unavoidable. In recognition of this, I have put together this collection of nine profiles and interviews, each with a "Commentary," or "story behind the story," attached. My purpose is to reveal the "task," "interest," and "point of view," as Popper put it, that went into the making of each article.

I chose these articles as representative of the best of my magazine profiles over the past decade. I have put them in chronological order, the most recent first, because that seemed a logical and democratic arrangement. And I have tried, by going over my carefully preserved notes and tapes and by delving into memory, to come up with an honest account of how I chose each subject, why, and what I did to write each piece. I hope that both general readers curious about how reporters work and my fellow journalists will enjoy this peek at the practical and ethical dilemmas a reporter faces while researching, interviewing, and writing profiles.

H.B.
New York, 1990

PORTRAITS IN PRINT

What are your historical Facts; still more your biographical? Wilt thou know a Man, above all a Mankind, by stringing-together beadrolls of what thou namest Facts?
—THOMAS CARLYLE, 1834,
*History of Frederick II of Prussia
Called Frederick the Great.*

■

THE POWER OF THE PROFILE

"This is a real literary form, the portrait. You can make anything you want out of it."

When Susan Sontag spoke these words to me, while I was interviewing her for *New York Woman*, I was struck by their insight. Because profiles are portraits of human beings, and human beings can understand each other only through the filter of their own perceptions, profiles are more subjective than any other form of journalism. Profile writers, therefore, are unusually free to create whatever image of that human being they want. This freedom has been recognized for some time by writers of full-length biographies, but few reporters realize that it applies as much to the journalist writing profiles as to the biographer writing tomes.

Many journalists don't like hearing about this freedom. They have been trained to deny their subjectivity, not to rely upon it. Some are even frightened by their power to make a judgment of someone and put it on the page, where it will be taken as fact. And they should be, for they are dictating how that person will be seen by the world. In a sense, profile writers are like critics, only instead of reviewing plays or movies, they are reviewing people. That is a much more direct and intimate power than all but the most political of journalists are used to having.

Intrinsic to the power to review people is another power that worries journalists, the power to hurt. This power exists in all forms of journalism—an essentially nosy, intrusive profession—but nowhere is it as acute as in profiles, for they deal with the private life, personality, and appearance of a subject more intimately than any other type of story. Profile writers are always having to decide which secrets to leave in and which to leave out. In addition, profile writers tend to become unusually close to their subjects because of the prolonged and personal nature of the interviews, and then to get tangled in the obligations of friendship. The result is that a writer's inclination to be kind often clashes with his or her duty to be fair. Biographer Leon Edel touched on this point when he wrote, "biographers must struggle constantly not to be taken over by their subjects, or to fall in love with them."[1] Tom Wolfe, in the introduction to his collection *The New Journalism*, went even further. Speaking of the friendship that can develop between reporter and subject, he wrote that reporters can "become stricken with a sense of guilt, responsibility, obligation." Wolfe's solution: "A writer needs at least enough ego to believe that what he is doing as a writer is as important as what anyone he is writing about is doing and that therefore he shouldn't compromise his own work. If he doesn't believe that his own writing is one of the most important activities going on in contemporary civilization, then he ought to move on to something else he thinks is . . . become a welfare eligibility worker or a clean-investment counselor for the Unitarian Church. . . ."[2]

All this power—to judge, to portray, to betray—is, of course, mitigated by the obligation to be accurate. Admittedly the subjects, by agreeing to be profiled, have consented to some extent to open up, to allow themselves to be examined, picked over, judged—painted. But that consent does not license writers to do as they wish. Profile writers have the artistic license to recreate people, not to create them from scratch—even the most experimental of the New Journalists acknowledged this. Profile writers therefore have to balance three factors: their private reaction to the subject, their duty to be fair, and their obligation to be accurate.

DEFINITION OF A PROFILE

When I use the word "profile," I am not talking about a question-and-answer interview, nor a standard newspaper-style interview, the kind which covers only a current subject: an interview with a governor about his next campaign, say, or with an author about her latest book. I define a profile as a complete portrait, with the following ingredients:

- Interviews with the subject.
- Life history of the subject.
- Description of the subject's person, home, and/or workplace.
- Interviews with sources close to the subject, such as family, friends, colleagues, employees, or fellow travelers.
- Interviews with critics or enemies.
- A theme: either a significant insight into the subject or a point of larger, symbolic value.

Again, this recipe can be summarized by the painting analogy. Imagine an old, yellowing oil of a man in his study. The corners are dark and shadowy, and the muted colors of mahogany furniture and Persian rugs blend into the walls—background details which lend color and mood to the piece. In the center is a desk covered with scientific instruments, and in the corner a woman hovers anxiously by the door—figures and objects which suggest something about the man. The man himself sits at the desk, his head in his hands, his body bent with fatigue. He is posed to reveal himself or the point the artist wishes to make about him. Every flake of paint—every word—counts. It tells a story. And although profile writers are not fictionalizing the way painters might, they are still balancing, selecting and placing every ingredient, all to add up to the portrait they want.

SELECTING THE SUBJECT

"There has rarely passed a life of which a judicious and faithful narrative would not be useful," wrote Samuel Johnson.[3]

I have to say right here, as undemocratic as it may sound, that I don't agree with Johnson that every person is worthy of a profile. Some people are not so interesting for themselves as for the work they do. A leading expert on cancer research may turn out to be a quiet family man with a crushingly dull background, but his knowledge is phenomenal. He is therefore better as an expert source for a story on cancer than as the subject of a profile. Other people are unsuitable for profiles simply because they cannot express themselves, even colloquially—in journalist's jargon, they make a terrible quote. Yet others are simply too boring—so boring that even a John McPhee would steer clear. All in all, a profile subject must make a good story: the plot should be exciting, the dialogue sharp, and the subject matter intriguing.

The reasons profile writers pick a particular subject fall into five general categories.

Fame. The person is a celebrity whom everyone is curious about. This could be the kind of "celebrity profile" of someone like Phoebe Snow or Princess Diana that runs every month in *Ladies' Home Journal.* Or it could be a more biting approach, such as the one Barbara L. Goldsmith took in her eerie portrait of Viva ("La Dolce Viva"), written for *New York* magazine at the height of Andy Warhol's hold over the counterculture in 1968.[4]

Achievement. This person has achieved something good—she's created the first magazine for black businesswomen, perhaps, or published a book, turned up a discovery, survived a disaster, found a cure. Or the achievement could be a bad thing—the person has murdered sixteen little boys. The point is that the reader wants to know what made the subject able to do this deed—what makes the subject tick. One of my favorites in this category is John Hersey's storylike portrait of Jessica Kelley, a "delicate little old widow" who survived a dangerous flood in 1955.[5]

Dramatization. This type of subject has a life that illustrates a larger issue, such as the effect of poverty, oppression, drugs, or AIDS on people's lives. Examples: single mothers, Vietnam vets, cancer victims, wives of murderers, prostitutes, refugees, and various types of survivors. One of my favorite pieces in Wolfe's collection of New Journalism falls into this category—a quiet portrait of a girl's life and death on a macrobiotic diet, "Beth Ann and Macrobioticism" by Robert Christgau.[6] In simple, unpretentious prose, Christgau portrayed through this unfortunate woman a uniquely 1960s version of American fanaticism.

Unusual lifestyles. The category portrays people whose lives inspire readers with fascination or envy. A portrait of the Amish, for example, or of life inside a palace. Good examples are Hunter S. Thompson's *The Hell's Angels*[7] and Frances Fitzgerald's portrait of the Rajneeshpuram cult in Oregon.[8] This type of profile may concentrate on one person to illustrate a lifestyle, or on a group of people. It was a favorite form for New Journalists such as Joan Didion and Tom Wolfe.

The Symbol. This sort of subject may not be particularly dramatic, but his or her life and personality symbolize a significant, or at least interesting, phenomenon. Perhaps he is a janitor, and the writer wishes to illustrate the work conditions of such a job through him. Or a cobbler, living a way of life that may not be around much longer. Perhaps he is a pickpocket or is homeless. Or perhaps the subject is a pioneer—a single mother who likes it that way, and finds life without a man simpler and more fun. Jane Kramer chose a subject like this for her profile *The Last Cowboy*.[9] She portrayed a fairly unremarkable man whose main claim to originality was that he was trying to live the life of an old-fashioned cowboy. In describing his loneliness and his battle against the modern, Kramer made the point that the last American frontier has been forever crossed.

A common mistake among beginning profile writers is to fall for the eccentricity trap. Not every kook makes a good profile; so it is important to ask if the subject's story is worth twenty pages or is just a party anecdote. I fell into the eccentricity trap myself as a student. Fresh over from England, I spent weeks on a profile of a therapist who wore bright clothes and specialized in treating people for writer's block. It was only when my professor pointed out that this was Berkeley, where there are more therapists than trees, that I realized I had confused my naïve fascination with California ways with a good profile subject.

Once the writer has chosen a subject, he or she must still hold that subject up to certain tests. It is most disheartening to spend weeks or even months on a profile only to realize that it has become boring. It is even more disheartening to spend those weeks on a profile and suddenly realize you don't know why you are doing it. I try to avoid this by asking myself early on whether my subject's story will fascinate, move, horrify, educate, amuse, or spark any recognition on the part of my readers. Why am I bothering to tell the story? Why publish the story now and not last year or next? And am I writing this story out of simple curiosity or because I think I can make something deeper out of it? This last question is the hardest and touches on a question that lies behind all journalism: is the need to know—or mere curiosity—enough justification for intruding on someone's privacy, or is a larger justification required? T. S. Eliot once wrote that "the line between curiosity which is legitimate and that which is merely harmless, and between that which is merely harmless and that which is vulgarly impertinent, can never be precisely drawn."[10] Perhaps that line can be drawn only by writers who question themselves over each story, or who are as confident as Tom Wolfe recommends.

I choose the subjects of my profiles for a mixture of motives but often simply because I admire their work. Susan Sontag appealed to me because of her position as a highly intellectual, respected, and independent woman in America; one who belonged neither to academia nor to any one category of writer. Joseph Brodsky drew me as an exile from his country and his language, and because I was moved by the bitter irony of that condition for a poet. Isaac Bashevis Singer intrigued me because he seemed like a living representative of a virtually extinct culture, a remnant of history, of the Polish Jews. Jessica Mitford attracted me because her work inspired me to become a journalist in the first place. In some cases I didn't really know why I had chosen a subject until I had done my research and found an aspect of them that hooked me. With Beverly Sills, for example, I started off merely curious to meet a star, but that curiosity deepened when I began to think about what mystery makes some people stars and others ordinary. I usually choose writers to profile because I write myself and so am always interested in how others do it; in other words, because I hope to learn from them. But other authors of profiles may choose their subjects for very different reasons—because they are fascinated by the underdog (A. J. Liebling's collection *The Jollity Building*), because they're out to expose wrongdoing (Joan Didion's "Bureaucrats"),[11] or because they're touched by ordinary people with ordinary problems (John Hersey's "The Brilliant Jughead").[12]

DIFFERENT APPROACHES

The kind of profile I do—the kind I have included in this collection —represents only a small range of the approaches one can take to writing profiles. I tend to rely on two or three interviews with the subject, interviews with other people who know the subject, and a lot of reading. Most of my pieces were written in under three months, and most written for magazines with style and word limits. Above all, they were not written as either budding or complete books. Other writers, especially those who have the financial support, word length, and time granted by an affiliation with the *New Yorker*, use other methods.

John McPhee often bases his profiles on a situation rather than the personality of one individual. He concentrates on describing events and surroundings, and in doing so, profiles a central character in the environment almost incidentally. In his much-admired "Travels in Georgia,"[13] for example, the reader gets to know the main character, Carol Ruckdeschel—a woman who picks dead animals off the road and eats them—only gradually, through the details of her work and lifestyle. McPhee takes months, if not years, to complete his research. Jane Kramer, whose portraits of people and their families in her book *Unsettling Europe* read like short stories, spends enough time with people to be able to enter their minds, it seems, and spill their thoughts aloud on the page. Other writers build portraits through research that never includes interviews with the actual subject: Janet Flanner was known for this at the *New Yorker*, and John Hersey did a brilliant profile of Robert Capa without meeting him by building him up in the way Capa had built himself—through other people's myths and stories about him. (Hersey opened that story with the wonderful line, "Capa, the photographer who is credited by his colleagues and competitors with having taken some of the greatest pictures of the Second World War, does not exist.")[14] Joan Didion has done some portraits based on one meeting (the Doors in her essay "The White Album")[15] and others based on nothing but reading and her own knowledge of the social milieu (her *New York Review of Books* essay on Nancy Reagan).[16]

Preparing the Onslaught

When I was battling the world press for Isaac Bashevis Singer's attention, in the wake of his Nobel prize, I used a much preached but rarely practiced journalistic technique which gave me a real advantage—I prepared. While other reporters were leaping in with stock questions about what he was going to do with the money and how he felt about winning, I got hold of an early copy of his new book, *Shosha*, from his publisher, read it, and questioned him about it. He was astonished. "Already you have read it?" he said, his eyebrows raised. "I did not even know it was out yet." I have found that if I read everything I can find about my subject before I start interviewing, I have a head start over many a lazier colleague.

Preparation is especially important when interviewing someone who has been in the press many times before. When I was reading over other people's interviews with Singer, for example, I found that he had a stock set of anecdotes he used over and over again, so I tried to find questions that would make him say something new. In preparing for the Sontag profile, I discovered that her interviews suddenly became more personal and dramatic after her bout with cancer and decided to elicit that frankness again by reopening the subject. The point is that by reading previous interviews with my sources, I found the original questions that startled them out of their boredom and won me a scoop. Sometimes, I even won some respect from my jaded subject, too.

Also, I always make sure to do some thorough library research before any interview, in order to master my subject's biography. *Current Biography, Who's Who, The Guide to Periodical Literature, The New York Times Index*, newspaper clip files, and the *Wilson Disk Indexes* are all valuable reference works. There's nothing like a reporter coming to do an in-depth interview and asking basic questions like "Where were you born?" to irritate an oft-interviewed subject.

My final stage of preparation is to write down a list of my questions. I write down every one, even "How old are you?" and "What is your telephone number?" because I find that during an interview, between the listening, the analyzing, the thinking of the next question, the observing, and the worrying about the tape recorder, I am so absorbed that it is easy to forget the obvious questions. To have to call back after a four-hour interview to ask someone's age is embarrassing. When I interviewed Jessica Mitford, I even wrote down "See toilet" in my list of questions because I had heard that her bathroom was plastered with hilarious advertisements from funeral-industry magazines such as *Casket and Sunnyside* and *Mortuary Management*, which she had collected during her research for *The American Way of Death*. (It was, and a rewarding trip to the toilet I had. One of the best was a sincere man saying, "Nothing else gives me the complete drainage that Frigid Plasma Co. does.") When I interviewed Susan Sontag, I brought along four single-spaced pages of questions. I wasn't able to ask them all, but it was a way of avoiding panic and controlling the interview.

THE INTERVIEW

The Big Apple Circus in New York once featured a team of Chinese jugglers who could each spin eight plates at a time on the ends of long, slender sticks. Interviewing is a similar balancing act. The reporter must listen, think, remember, connect, analyze, observe, invent the next question, judge, and record all at once. At the end of a two-hour interview, if it has gone well, the reporter should be exhausted. I remember reeling out of my interview with Joseph

Brodsky, feeling as if I'd been in his apartment for days (although it was only about two and a half hours). I was drained and literally giddy with fatigue. The concentration and energy it takes to engage someone in a one-sided, significant, and revealing conversation should never be underestimated. For this reason, I use a tape recorder (one with a loud stopping noise), I always plug it in (never rely on batteries), and I pause a few times during the interview to go over my list of questions, awkward silence and all, to make sure nothing is forgotten.

I also insist on seeing subjects at home whenever possible. People's homes tell so much about them. Brodsky, for instance, lives in a poky basement apartment, dark and gloomy, with two resplendent pieces of furniture that dominate everything else—an elaborate antique desk, covered with photographs, and a gigantic wastepaper basket in the shape of a Coca-Cola can. That combination of austere Old World and crass new Americana gave me hints about Brodsky's attitude to his exile. In contrast, Jessica Mitford's home was awash in papers, books, furniture, old mugs—it looked as if twenty people lived there. And indeed, Mitford and her husband are the types who open their homes to neighbors, friends, and political comrades.

If it is relevant to the story, I try to see the subject's workplace, too. But I avoid interviewing in cafés and restaurants because it is hard to listen or record over the hubbub, hard to ask intelligent questions with my mouth full of fish, and even harder to add knives and forks to the eight or nine plates I am already juggling. Plus, the waiter inevitably interrupts just as my subject is about to confess he really was a Nazi collaborator.

I always snoop. There's no point being in the subject's home if I am not going to look at it. I snoop, peek, examine, observe as much as I can, and then I get into the bathroom during a break in the interviewing and write down everything my tape recorder can't catch or that my memory will soon lose: the pictures on the walls, the period of the furniture, the color of the rugs, the knickknacks on the coffee table. A subject's home reveals that subject's taste, and taste reveals character, class, education, politics, and individuality. John Gregory Dunne is perhaps the most shameless snoop of all. In his book *Harp* he extolls the virtues of rifling through other people's medicine cabinets. By examining their pill bottles and birth control devices, he explains, "entire medical, social and sexual histories can be constructed."[17]

I consciously look at my subject, as well. It is surprising how easy it is to forget to do this when I am busy listening. I try to remind myself to get the color of his hair and eyes right, and the color of her pantsuit. ("Dear Helen," Mitford wrote to me after my profile of her was published. "Thanks so much for your article. There was a wee bit of jumping up & down at the lead para . . . bright pink pantsuit, which I thought of as a muted mushroom color?") I have learned to expect to be disagreed with, but if I am sure it was bright pink, I feel safe. I try to notice my subject's habits, too—the way he sits, smokes, sweeps back his hair, fiddles. I look at how my subject holds her eyebrows and mouth, what he has inscribed on his T-shirt, the endearments she calls her spouse. When I arrived early at the hotel room where Singer was hiding out from journalists in the aftermath of his Nobel prize, I overheard him quarreling with his wife. Her native language is German, his Yiddish; so, I discovered, they fight in English.

At the beginning of the interview, the reporter must of course win the trust of subjects and help them relax, whether that reporter is after dirt or just a kindly portrait. For this reason I try not to interrupt a lot, especially at first, unless the subjects repeat themselves or go off on endless digressions. And I avoid bringing up the delicate or challenging too early. Jessica Mitford wrote in her excellent guide to investigative reporting, *Poison Pensmanship*, that questions should progress from the kind to the cruel. In order to avoid killing off the interview before it gets started, I save the challenges until the end, when I already have a few yards of quotable material safely on tape.

But controlling the interview also means weaving together the complicated network of the subject's answers. A question I asked in hour one might not get answered until hour three, and then in a different context. For this reason I have to keep alert, and I refer constantly to my written questions so that I can steer the conversation back to the topic I want. If this means stopping one train of thought and switching to another, I do so. It may not be smooth conversational technique, but it can save me hours of listening to off-the-track waffling.

I listen. I never would have expected to have to say that until I had a taste of being on the other side during a book tour. I was astonished at how many radio and television reporters talked more than I did when they were interviewing me. Journalism is not a job for big egos—reporters must suppress their opinions and urge to show off and sit at the feet of other people. It is a humble profession while you are interviewing—the power comes once you hit the page.

Finally, I always close by asking for another interview. To do a thorough profile, one interview is never enough. I find I need to follow up on all the questions and interesting leads I may have missed the first time.

During an interview, the reporter is a receiver. This means you must concentrate on getting your subjects to open up, to forget you and to talk to themselves if need be, while you listen. Although a friendly response will help to warm the reporter, it is not necessary to the interview. When I interviewed the writer Paule Marshall, for instance, she seemed much more comfortable talking to the wall than to me, off in her own memories and musings. I listened, recorded, and observed, but rarely met her eyes. That told me something about her, or about her and me, but it didn't make the interview a failure.

After the Interview

As soon as I leave my subject, I make a beeline for the nearest café or restaurant, before I have time to be distracted by anything new, and write down everything I remember from the moment I saw my subject's front door to the moment I entered the café. I record it in narrative form and chronological order, for that helps me organize my articles when I come to write. I am usually longing for a glass of wine or a beer by that time to unwind with, but I resist until my memory has unburdened itself onto the page.

Then I break a journalistic rule and ask myself, "Do I like this person? Do I trust this person?" And I go a step further and ask *why*. As I opened by saying, journalists must be aware of why they feel as they do about their subject because those feelings are going to creep into the story whether they like it or not. Being aware of their reactions to a subject is not only a way to keep an eye on their biases; it is a way of finding a window into the subject's personality. My reaction of distrust might lead me to an insight that will provide a theme for my piece, for example. Or my sense of dislike might tell me that my subject has a streak of arrogance, an important characteristic in an otherwise admirable person. I consider the examination of my judgment of the subject an essential part of my research. I may not include all these personal observations and speculations in the final draft, but they help me to interpret all I have learned. And I have found that, once I know my real opinion of the subject, I can temper it with the opinions of others.

Most of my leads have come from this initial scribbling, for it is the scenes, the unspoken moments, the subjective judgments, and the asides said after the tape is off that often give real life to a profile. Brodsky biting the filters off his cigarettes and throwing them into the fireplace, even though he'd been told not to smoke after his heart bypass. Mitford hopping on one leg in glee as her husband announces, "We've won." Sontag's rueful statement that she feels slapped in the face when people tell her she intimidates them. All these moments came from the notes I wrote right after the interview—from fresh, recorded memory, not from the tape.

I try to record every detail of my subject's face on paper, too, before I forget it. The memory is very short on visual detail, and I find that I often come up with my most accurate, telling descriptions when the person's face is still hovering before my eyes. I realized that the word for Sontag's laugh was "goofy" while I was sitting in a restaurant five minutes after I'd left her.

Finally, I transcribe my interviews as soon as possible, trying not to let more than a day pass. There are always murky words and muttered phrases that my memory has to supplement.

OTHER SOURCES

Profile writers must interview outside sources about their subject for several reasons: to achieve balance, so that the piece reads neither like public relations fluff nor like a raving attack; to supplement the subject's view of him or herself; to test the writer's own judgment, likes, and dislikes against those of others; and to provide expert opinions from within the subject's field (poets on another poet, for example, or critics on a writer)—opinions the journalist may not be qualified to proffer. I try to talk to the subject's spouse, children, friends, students, colleagues, employers, employees—above all to his or her critics or enemies—in order to get a variety of views and to see how many of them coincide with or contradict my own.

AWE

No writer can get to the meat of a subject's personality if he or she is too intimidated to ask penetrating questions, or too worried about sounding stupid. Adequate preparation can take care of some of this, but so can familiarity with the subject. My rule of thumb is, if my subjects scare me, I keep going back till they don't. I know of no other cure.

In some ways my best stories came out of people who initially awed me—Singer, Sontag, Brodsky, Mitford—because I had to persist with my interviewing until I broke through my awe to some understanding of them as actual people. There are some subjects with whom I have never felt at ease, true, but I was not, after all, trying to become their best friend.

WRITING

The moment has come. Sheafs of transcribed interviews litter my desk, and piles of notes threaten to bury my lap. I read them all through, put them aside for the time being, and think: what is this piece going to say?

After years of religiously following outlines, I find I do my best writing when I wheel free and write a first draft without even referring to my notes. Sometimes, to get over the "Oh God, The Lead" panic, I say to myself, what would I write if I wasn't even thinking of publication? I deliberately forget my editors, my readers, my subject, and think only of what I really want to say, as if I were writing a letter to a friend rather than an article. With the Sontag piece, knowing how many people would be reading and judging it, I tried to be purposely irreverent, just to get over my nerves. That's how I came up with "A lot of people are afraid of Susan Sontag," for I had been amused by the amount of trepidation people had about her and how unfrightening she really was. But when I wrote the line I never expected it to reach print.

My choice of lead will guide me through the rest of the piece; so I choose it with care. I may need to write a whole collection of leads before I can get any further. The lead not only sets the tone for the piece but introduces the theme—that insight or point I mentioned in the list of ingredients above. A good lead should fit in with the conclusion and foreshadow it. "A lot of people are afraid of Susan Sontag" was an appropriate introduction to my point about her public persona being so much more intimidating than her private one. "Joseph Brodsky looked out of place" fit in exactly with my picture of him as a rebel, an individualist sundered from home and language. In the Mitford piece I wanted to portray her and her husband as partners in their fight against injustice, so I used a scene rather than a statement and opened with him announcing his triumph in court and her reaction of glee.

The finding of the theme, which the lead will introduce, is essential to making an articulate, coherent article out of a package of unconnected notes. As Leon Edel put it, "a writer of lives must extract individuals from their chaos."[18] Profile writers are constrained to impose a pattern on their subjects' lives in order to make the writing manageable—profiles cannot meander around the way a real life might. But in choosing their theme, writers must be accurate.

When I search for my themes, I go back to those first questions I asked myself about the story. Why am I writing this? Why would anyone be interested? At this point, I rely more than ever on my subjective judgment of the subject, on my private reaction to him or her, and on my own interpretations of my research. In other words, I use my instincts and insights, the parts of me that go beyond journalistic training, and I fall back on all the social perceptions I've picked up throughout my life. My knowledge of the subject will have come a long way since I began the piece, but my theme is usually linked with the reasons I first wanted to do a story. I approached Beverly Sills to find out what made her famous and found that her determination applied to the private tragedies of her life, as well as to her ambition. I thought of Brodsky as an exile from his language and came to see him as a rebel against all forms of conformity. I approached Sontag thinking of her independence from categories but became intrigued by her "move toward the personal."

One danger in finding a theme is that the writer so falls in love with it that he or she begins to bend the facts to fit. This is a problem biographers have faced for decades. In Virginia Woolf's biography of Roger Fry, for example, she asked, "how can one cut loose from facts, when there they are, contradicting my theories?"[19] Arguably, the writers of literary biographies may have more artistic license in regard to this than people who pose as journalists, but on the whole a bender of facts will pay for it in the end by losing credibility.

The theme is introduced by the lead, and that theme should be the backbone of the story. Whether the writer chooses to structure the story chronologically or according to some more abstract scheme, the theme should provide a guide all the way through. There is no one formula on how to organize something as complex as a profile —the six ingredients can be put together in a variety of orders— but I find that if I let my theme guide me, the logic finds itself.

Once I have spurted out my first, unfettered draft and found my lead, I then go back to my notes and make my outline. Now begins the painstaking task of inserting accurate quotations and description, of choosing what to delete, of juggling, transposing, tightening —again, an impossible task without a theme to guide me. Most of my original draft may be gone by the end, but with luck the spirit of it will still be there. If nothing else, that original, spontaneous spurt may have found me the voice and tone to use for the piece, and that is no small achievement.

STYLE

> To deny biography the signature of a style, the sound of a single voice rather than the crowd-noise of the species Biographer, seems perverse, artless, and servile."
> —GEOFFREY WOLFF, *Minor Lives*[20]

I have noticed a certain inverse snobbery among some journalists who hold that nonfiction writers should look askance at "style," and think only of expressing themselves in the simple, clear English an eighth grader can understand. This may be all very well for newspapers, but not so for a profile. If there is no verve, no originality, no humor or music to one's writing, it will probably have no readers. And all that work will be for nought.

Almost any story can be made dull if written badly enough. "The body of James Jones, a factory worker, was found on Lido beach at 7:30 A.M. by Gloria Pinkerton, a thirty-five-year-old seamstress, when the two dogs she was walking along Lido beach on Tuesday morning scented the body and began to bark, leading her to the site of the body." I made that up, but it isn't far from the prose I see in certain newspapers every morning. A muddled, repetitive sentence like that is enough to make a reader lose interest even in a dead body.

There is a lot of confusion about what good writing is. Many people make the mistake of equating it with flowery writing: a profusion of words, a crowd of adjectives—fancy, show-offy stuff. We are warned fairly often about that these days. But another mistake, and a subtler one, is to go too far in the other direction and equate good writing with simple sentences and nothing else.

This is much in fashion now, not only in journalism but in fiction. True, clarity is the first requirement of journalistic writing: if readers can't understand what they are being told, they won't read on. But clarity doesn't just mean simplicity: "Dead. That's what James Jones was when Gloria Pinkerton found his body. Pinkerton had gone out to walk her dogs. Suddenly, one of them yelped. She followed it. A foot stuck out from behind a rock. 'It was a body,' she said, 'a body I knew.' "[21]

I admit there's a wacky humor in that, but this kind of staccato writing pays no attention to the logic of our language. We do not talk like that. We are not telegrams. Our language contains music and rhythms that we vary to reflect our moods. Rhythm makes us listen when a story is told, compels us to concentrate. Short sentences have a value when used for surprise, or to change a mood or rhythm, but if we write in jerky, short sentences all the time the effect on readers is like a hypnotic beat—it puts them to sleep.

Good writing also means being honest. Honest writing suits the subject and is not a disguise for an ego. It does not show off: "The sun shone dimly that morning on Lido beach, almost as if Nature herself knew something tragic had happened there the night before." It does not put the reporter before his subject, in what I call Look-at-Me journalism: "When this reporter got to Gloria Pinkerton, he found her shaken." And it does not try so hard to stand out that it practically bursts its britches: "We all share a nightmare. Maybe some of us grow out of it as we achieve maturity, maybe many of us don't. But we all know the fear that one day, when we are busily minding our own business, we might stumble across a corpse. Gloria Pinkerton lived that terror."

I know of no better way to develop a graceful style than to read the great authors of fiction and nonfiction, but Strunk and White's *Elements of Style* and William Zinsser's *On Writing Well* are two books every writer should use.

A word about description: it should be short, precise, and telling. A writer does best by picking out one or two startling details, rather than snowing the reader with lists of them and with adjectives or clichés. Clichés only blur people into a mass of rosy-cheeked women or handsome, square-jawed men. Tolstoy and Dickens are the two best describers I know. I read *War and Peace* years ago, but can still picture Pierre as a "bear" of a man, with a youthful, naïve manner. Tolstoy brings his characters to life not by endless detail but by a single, carefully chosen feature or mannerism, repeated many times. Levin in *Anna Karenina*, for instance, is always blushing and stroking his beard.

Metaphors are particularly useful in description. A writer can tell more about a man by saying he looks like a sleepy mole than by offering lines and lines about his small head and pointed nose and squinting eyes and brownish skin. A student of mine once wrote an entire page trying to describe an underground room through which a pipeline was being laid. When I said, "But what does the room look like?" she replied, "A shoebox," and finally I could see what she meant.

THE RECEPTION

Once a profile has survived endless rewrites, selling, editing, and publishing, it reaches the finale—the subject's reaction. My rule of thumb is that if the subject unreservedly loves it, I have failed, because no accurate, fair profile should be as rosy as the vanity we each have secreted in our hearts. I don't mean that writers should invite outrage and hatred, unless they are doing an exposé of an unqualified villain, but that we should expect objections, grumbles, or more commonly, a stony silence. Think of the portrait painter, wincing as the subject rails, "This doesn't look anything like me!" The writer has created a portrait in print, and like any artist, will have to face reviews. The best we can hope for is a shrug and a grudging admission that what we wrote was fair.

ONE

The Passionate Mind

■

PHOTOGRAPH © 1990, ANNIE LEIBOVITZ/CONTACT PRESS IMAGES.

SUSAN SONTAG

A lot of people are afraid of Susan Sontag. Getting to meet her is a bit like trying to meet Joan of Arc on her day off. "Oh, I don't know when we'll fit you in," say her publishers, whom Sontag has trained to be her guards. "She's going to Germany and Ireland this month" or "Oh, she'll never let you into her apartment." So when you dial her phone number and she actually answers, you feel tricked.

"I don't know what they think my life is like," Sontag says irritably in her deep, flat voice. "All I do is sit in my hot apartment all day and write." And she lets you into her apartment, which is actually cooled by a breeze from the elegant open patio, and not only greets you with a smile but makes you a cup of tea. "Some people are awkward with me," she acknowledges, standing in her kitchen. "When they come up to me and say, 'I admire your work, but you intimidate me,' I feel as if I've been slapped in the face. It's such an act of hostility."

People are intimidated by Sontag because she is one of the few humans in America who are famous for their intellect. Although she hates labels and distrusts the term *intellectual*, it fits her. Best known for her essays and pronouncements, she is a freelance intellectual and interpreter of culture—her essays have covered art, filmmakers, writers, photography, illness, and now AIDS—and as such, she has become recognized, even revered, throughout the world. As the critic John Simon wrote in 1984, "The polymath Susan Sontag exemplifies the main currents of New York thought."

People are also intimidated by Sontag's public persona. She is poised and comfortable in the spotlight (perhaps partly because she dabbled in acting as a child) and seems to relish arguing over issues, presiding at cultural events and taking part in international conferences. She is a member of such august societies as the American Academy and Institute of Arts and Letters and the New York Institute for the Humanities (a kind of lunch club for thinkers) and in 1987 raised her profile even higher by becoming president of PEN, the writers' organization.*

Yet it is ironic that Sontag is just now taking on the most public role of her life, for in all other ways she is moving toward the personal. The emotional aftermath of her breast cancer twelve years ago, the number of her friends now dying of AIDS, and her view of life from middle age seem to be pushing the formerly aloof Sontag to a new openness and intimacy, both in her lifestyle and in her work. Her forthcoming book is virtually a plea for the rights of AIDS victims, her most recent short stories are autobiographical, and now she is working on a novel and a memoir. "I don't want to do much more essay writing," she says with a touch of wistfulness. "I feel I can make better use of my talents by writing in a freer, more emotionally direct way. There must be some puritanism in me that has lashed me to the essay for so long; I find essays extremely difficult to write."

Sontag first became a celebrity at age thirty-one, when she wrote an essay, "Notes on 'Camp,'" defining and celebrating camp taste. Published in *Partisan Review* in 1964, the essay was immediately noticed and hailed, and almost overnight, it seemed, the image of this tall young woman draped in a curtain of black hair and gazing seriously out of intense, dark eyes became familiar. Sontag was the essence of the beat intellectual, posing makeupless for photographs in dark clothes and, in some pictures, not even wearing shoes. Ever since, the literati have been puzzling over how she became so hot so fast.

One theory is that her ideas were ripe for the times. She brought French postmodernist thinking to America in the sixties, when the intellectual world here was ready to break tradition, mock academia, experiment with language and form—to play games. She played those games well, and she played them young. In 1969 *Current Biography* touted her as "the darling—and, to some, the

---

* Since this writing, Sontag has retired from the presidency.

demon—of the New York intellectual establishment." In due course the press was throwing around all sorts of peculiar (and sexist) epithets about her: "Mary McCarthy's successor as the 'Dark Lady of American Letters,' " even "the Natalie Wood of the U.S. Avant-Garde."

Sontag dislikes thinking of herself as famous and says that when she thinks of her position, all she really sees is a "typewriter with a lot of paper beside it." Nevertheless, she is not above using her fame to take controversial stands, as when she attacked liberal dogma in 1982 with the statement that communism is "fascism with a human face." "I do have a taste for the adversarial role," she admits. "I am a public figure insofar as I have participated in public debate over things like the ERA and Vietnam and now PEN. I do so because I am civic-minded and I care about the fate of literacy and cultural life in my country." Sharon DeLano, a friend for more than ten years, puts it another way. "Susan," she says, "is fierce."

Because Sontag is so visible as an intellectual—let alone as one who dares to comment on politics—she has naturally drawn criticism over the years. Academics in particular accuse her of not being an original thinker. They say that she has merely translated French ideas for popular American consumption and has sacrificed serious thought for trendiness. "She can either do justice to the subtlety of the thinker in question and increase his following by a very few," wrote Princeton professor David Bromwich in a 1980 book review, "or reduce him to manageable slogans and greatly increase the frequency with which his name occurs in the intellectual chatter of the age. She has chosen the latter course."

The charge of trendiness infuriates Sontag. "I wrote about some things no one else was writing about—then people came along and said what I'd done was trendy," she says. "And this accusation is one of the reasons I rarely write about contemporary things anymore. I thought I was performing a public service, sharing the pleasure of discovering things, but if I'm going to be accused of being trendy, to hell with it."

At the age of fifty-five Sontage hasn't changed much since her early days of fame. She is thicker around the hips and likes to make jokes about avoiding the refrigerator, but she still has the grace of a tall, strong woman imbued with self-confidence. Her face tends to look pale and tired, but when she smiles—a big, rather goofy smile that contrasts strikingly with her normally somber expression—she suddenly loses twenty years and looks again the lively, handsome woman whom the critic Herbert Mitgang once called a literary pinup. Her hair is only to her shoulders now, but it is still heavy and black, except for the famous spray of white by her temple. And however imperious, even stern, her public demeanor may be, in private she can still relax into intimate conversation.

One of the questions that most amuses her, for example, is whether she shuns makeup for political reasons. "Oh, no," she answers, laughing. "I don't wear makeup because I feel attractive enough without it. If I ever feel I'm not, which may happen in about five minutes, I'll start wearing it. But I think it's wonderful that people try to make themselves beautiful." She leans forward on her patio couch, legs splayed, an elbow on each knee. "I dye my hair, for instance. I was beginning to have gray hair and had a white streak, and then when I had cancer and chemotherapy my hair fell out, as everyone's does, temporarily. When it grew back, it was very gray, as often happens. I was in my early forties." She shrugs. "For about a year I said, 'This is my hair, this is what it is,' but I didn't like it. So I dyed it but left the white streak." She grabs the lock of white hair, twists it and holds it up. "They put the white streak up like a unicorn, you see, wrapped with tinfoil, and dye the rest. I have to dye it every six weeks, but I still like looking the way I used to look." Dropping the hair, she falls back on the couch, puts her feet on the glass coffee table, and chuckles.

Sontag's new book, *AIDS and Its Metaphors*, reflects the concern with illness that she developed when she found she had breast cancer. The book is a sequel to *Illness as Metaphor*, the essay that Sontag thought up while in the hospital. Both books describe how patients with stigmatized diseases such as cancer, and now AIDS, are blamed for their sickness through the language used to discuss illness and by the attitudes of doctors and governments. Sontag argues that this blame makes us believe that illness is a deserved punishment and so we become too passive and accepting to fight for better research or treatment. "I thought that if you could make people more aware of these self-punishing stereotypes, you would actually free people to seek better treatment," she says. "I felt I was coming to the aid of people who are punished by vindictive and irrational attitudes."

Illness as Metaphor came as a surprise to Sontag's readers. Her earlier writings had been mostly impersonal. Both in essays and in fiction she had kept herself in the background—something that in a man would have passed without comment but that, in her case, probably added to the public perception of her as cold. Even in interviews she maintained a distance, rarely referring to her private life or past, and today in conversation she still uses the words *you* or *one* more than *I*. But in the *Illness* book she was quite different. Suddenly the distant Ms. Cool was not only personal but angry—so angry that she was telling people what they couldn't say. Now she is about to do it again in her book on AIDS.

"I am a crusader about the ill," she says. "Once you've experienced being mortally ill and you've come back, you have learned something that's worth knowing." She lifts her feet down from the coffee table, frowns at her hands, and settles into a thought. "When you find out that you are ill," she continues, "your priorities are shattered. One moment you are in a boat, and the next moment you are in the water. But if you can take in the idea that you're going to die, there is a euphoria in it as well as great terror. Nothing else is real except the most intense experiences, so you reach out for intimacy. It can be exalting, even as you are reduced to this damaged body that is being cut up and made ugly and made to hurt and feel vulnerable. But it's passionate and turbulent and intense." She pauses, takes off her clear plastic watch and rebuckles it.

"I have friends dying right now of AIDS," she adds quietly. "I'm visiting two of them. And I feel a competence to be with them, to touch them, hold them, sit and talk about what they are going through and speak of death." She looks up, dark eyes flashing. "Of course, they're dying and I'm not; nevertheless, I have been where they are, and I'm not frightened." (The next morning Sontag was called to the side of one of these friends. She spent four days and nights by his bed, going home only to snatch a few hours of sleep, until the fifth day, when he died.)

Sontag discovered her own illness in the course of a routine checkup when she was forty-two. She subsequently went through five operations, stringent doses of chemotherapy, and a mastectomy, and she was told that she would die.

"She got very angry at the way doctors talked to her about the cancer," says her thirty-six-year-old son, David Rieff. "She knew that she had to fight." She read everything she could find about the disease, he says, and met with foreign doctors to have them explain all the latest theories. Finally she took herself off to France for the treatment she could get nowhere else. "And the fact of the matter is that what she got twelve years ago people are getting normally here now, so she was right."

The successful, all-out fight that Sontag waged against her cancer revealed the "avidity" that, Rieff says, characterizes all of her life. "She has a kind of steely optimism. I don't mean anything naïve, but she has an almost unslakable kind of curiosity, of interest in the world. She is someone who can go to an opera, meet someone at two in the morning to go to the Ritz and listen to some neo-Nazi punk synthesizer band, and then get up the next morning to see two Crimean dissidents. I think a lot of her strength as an intellectual has to do with that kind of insistence, curiosity, and appetite."

Rieff speaks of his mother as one would of a mentor or perhaps a big brother, and except for their physical resemblance—he is also tall and dark, with the same loose-limbed, clumsy grace—it is hard to imagine him as her son. There is a good reason for this, as he explains. Sontag gave birth to him when she was only nineteen, having married his father, sociologist Philip Rieff, at seventeen, and their closeness in age eventually made them close in friendship. That closeness increased when she left her husband, at twenty-six, took David to New York, and brought him up alone.

"We lived in a kind of amiable squalor for a long time till she got a bit of money lateish in my childhood," Rieff recalls in his English-tinted drawl. "She didn't cook. Oh, there was the occasional game attempt to fry this or that, but it wasn't convincing to either of us, so we ate out a lot. My main memory is of our talks, a certain kind of impassioned conversation on any conceivable subject that took place against all sorts of backdrops. Intellectual conversation had almost the same quality as emergencies for us—you put aside whatever mood you were in to talk.

"And then there were her friends," Rieff adds. "Jasper Johns, Joseph Chakin, and others, which we sort of shared. Susan and Jonathan Miller and Oliver Sacks used to go to autopsies together."

Autopsies? Was this not a rather serious, even gloomy, household?

"I think it was," Rieff muses. "I think I'm the one who brought the humor in. But we were serious without being solemn. Even when Susan was ill there were high times. A lot of irreverence. And we went clothes shopping a lot."

Did he ever call her Mommy? "Oh," he says, waving an arm

bedecked with an elaborate Indian turquoise bracelet, "there was a time. I sort of ended it at a preposterously early point. It always seemed a bit forced to me."

His mother laughs when told this. "That's not true! He stopped calling me Mommy at about fifteen, not at a preposterously early age. And I didn't like it. I said, 'There's no other person in the world who's ever going to call me Mommy, so please don't stop.' He said, 'I won't call you Mommy.' I said, "I won't let you call me Susan,' so we went through close to a year in which he called me 'Hey!' " She laughs again. "But we are so close, so fond of each other, that we've had to grow careful over the years. We live in the same world, have many of the same interests; so keeping some separateness was an achievement for both of us, and one not done without difficulty."

These days Sontag is surprisingly frank about herself and her life. She not only glows with pride about her son but speaks warmly of her newfound closeness with her sister, calls herself an addict of intimacy, and bemoans the perpetual lack of money that has forced her to write "short" instead of devoting two or three years to one long book as she would like. "Shorter forms—stories and essays— get published in magazines and I get paid, which makes it possible to pay the rent," she says. "It's as simple as that."

Money has long been a problem for Sontag, and she bristles quickly at any assumption that she is rich. She only rents her downtown duplex, she emphasizes, and most of her travels are paid for by the various conferences she attends. At the time of her illness she didn't even have insurance, so Robert Silvers, an old friend and the coeditor of the *New York Review of Books*, had to rally friends to pay for her treatment. She lacks money, she says, because she is not the kind of writer whose books make much, and because she won't teach or write journalism. "I don't because it makes it very hard for me to concentrate, to hear my own voice. I need to stay home all day and just let it all swim around in my head."

At home Sontag keeps her daily routine simple: rising early, making her "stupid coffee," avoiding the phone and the refrigerator, and writing. She tries not to go out to lunch and saves all her chores for Fridays, in order to interrupt as little of the week as possible.

"Work is like a child," she says. "It will take as much time as you give it. Because of that there have been periods in my life when I have accepted solitude. I don't think I've chosen it, I've only accepted it. But I persist in thinking that one should be able to mate and have children and intimate friendships and, if you're lucky, loving relationships with your family and still be able to work."

In the evenings Sontag sees a friend for dinner, a movie, ballet, or a concert—such friends as Elizabeth Hardwick; poets Joseph Brodsky and Richard Howard; her publisher, Roger Straus; and many others in and out of the arts, famous and otherwise. She says she lives in Manhattan ("this boat anchored off the coast of the United States") because of its "cultural smorgasbord" and because of her friends and her son. "My favorite situation is sitting and talking with one other person," she says. "I dislike literary parties and openings because every time I'm in a conversation, somebody interrupts us. I'm too hungry for that one-on-one situation."

Sontag traces this hunger for intimacy back to an isolated childhood—her parents were often abroad, her father died when she was five, and her mother was emotionally remote. But that need and the move toward the personal in Sontag's work may also have a lot to do with her brush with death.

"When I got sick, I wanted to be closer to people, to accept consolation and talk about life and death," she says. "For the sake of my self-respect I continued to work, but if I were a less conscious, driven person, I would have simply been with people. I didn't want to write—I wanted to hold hands."

"Of course, I *am* a writer," she adds. "I can't imagine not being a writer any more than I can imagine not being a woman. But being a writer isn't the most important thing to me. The most important thing is . . . how to say it?" She frowns. "The most important thing is one's inner life." She pauses again, revising. "The most important thing is one's connection with other people."

SUSAN SONTAG

PERSONAL

Born New York City, January 16, 1933.

Raised in Tucson, Arizona, and Los Angeles.

Mother: schoolteacher; father: salesman; younger sister: businesswoman in Hawaii.

Married Philip Rieff, an instructor whom she met at the University of Chicago when she was seventeen and he was twenty-eight; they divorced nine years later; one child, David Rieff, born 1952, author and former editor at Farrar, Straus, and Giroux (edited, among others, Philip Roth, Joseph Brodsky and Susan Sontag).

EDUCATION

Started school at age six in third grade because she could already read and write; graduated North Hollywood High School at fifteen; B.A. from University of Chicago, 1951; M.A from Harvard (completing all work for a Ph.D. except dissertation).

WRITINGS

Among her works: *Against Interpretation* (1966); *Death Kit,* a novel (1967); *Styles of Radical Will* (1969); *Duet for Cannibals,* screenplay produced in Sweden (1970); *I, etcetera,* short stories (1978); *On Photography* (1977); *Illness as Metaphor* (1978); *Under the Sign of Saturn* (1980); *A Susan Sontag Reader* (1982). Editor of *Selected Writings of Artaud* (1976) and *A Barthes Reader* (1982).

PERSONAL STYLE

Elegant, but never seen in a dress. "I love clothes," she says. Her friend Sharon DeLano isn't so sure: "Susan's not very interested in sports, television, or clothes. Just look at the way she dresses."

LEAST FAVORITE THINGS

Being asked why she married at seventeen: "You're asking me to make myself into an object."

Being labeled a writer about popular culture. "When I was young, I made a flip remark about the Supremes being as interesting as Jasper Johns, and ever since, people have had this mental cliché that I write about popular culture. I do nothing of the kind."

FAVORITE THINGS

Dinner with one other person; lending books to a friend; collecting books and eighteenth-century prints; her son.

SONTAG COMMENTARY

N ew York Woman asked me to profile Susan Sontag at the beginning of a busy summer. Intrigued that a women's magazine would be interested in someone so literary, I eagerly went to meet the editors in their plush American Express–supported offices on Sixth Avenue. It wasn't long before I began to feel alarm as well as excitement. "Find out if she dyes her hair," one of the editors commanded, waving a beringed hand, "and tell us all about her sex life."

Now, my idea of the way to approach a heavyweight intellectual like Sontag was neither to do an exposé on her latest bedmate nor a chatty column about her makeup preferences. In my opinion those approaches were both trivial and sexist. Nevertheless, I also knew I couldn't do a *Paris Review*–style interview on her latest literary theories either, not for a slick women's magazine. The trick was to find a balance, and I had to get to know Sontag before I could find it.

The first step was to get her to cooperate. Writers often find themselves in a Catch 22 here—the subject won't agree to the interview unless a magazine has commissioned it, and the magazine won't commission it until the subject agrees. This is usually solved by a series of promises—the magazines assures conditional interest so that you can approach the subject, the subject conditionally agrees, the magazine at last commits, the subject likewise, and eventually you have a contract. But getting Sontag's cooperation looked impossible, because from the moment I approached her minions to obtain her unlisted telephone number, they balked.

The only reason Sontag would agree to the interview, I knew, was that her new book, *AIDS and Its Metaphors*, was coming out that winter. Normally, publishers are only too eager to have their authors interviewed at such a time, for authors on the whole get little attention for their books, but because Sontag also uses her publisher as her agent and bodyguard, the usual rules did not apply. I was told firmly that I would have to write Sontag a letter and submit clips of my previous work before I could be considered as a possible interviewer. And even then, they said, I wouldn't be allowed in her apartment, I'd have to wait a long time to catch her between trips abroad, and they could not guarantee her willingness anyway. Sontag's publicists, whose job is to promote her, were instead protecting her, and this paradox amused me. The seeds of my lead were already in place: "A lot of people are afraid of Susan Sontag."

I dutifully wrote my letter and sent my clips, and after I passed the test the publicists' voices warmed. Finally I was allowed to telephone the queen bee herself, and she answered the phone like any old person. I apologized for disturbing her and, in the light of all her publicists had said, asked her anxiously when she would be free. "I don't know what they think my life is like," she replied irritably. "All I do is sit in this hot apartment all day and write." Not only did she invite me to her apartment, but she gave me meticulous directions to it. I realized that somewhere there was a missing link between the normal writer trying to work and a bevy of fans and editorial assistants regarding her an unapproachable. As contradictions and paradoxes are often the meat of journalism, I was already on my way.

After several weeks of reading Sontag's many books and essays, and the even more plentiful articles about her that I dug out from library clip files, the *New York Times*, and the *Periodical Index*, I had learned a few more important things about interviewing Sontag. The first was that her interviewers tended to spend a great deal of time talking about how they were intimidated by her ("Look at Me" journalism). The second was that, with the exception of a facetious *People* magazine story, no one had really attempted to profile her but only to review or interview her. And the third was that she was at her most human, and most revealing, when interviewed on the subject of her cancer.

Since I had a couple of weeks before the first interview, I began by approaching other sources first. I had been unwilling to do this initially, for fear that she would get wind of it and be offended, but scheduling forced me. I knew through the publishing grapevine that her son, David Rieff, was her editor at Farrar, Straus, and Giroux; so he was easy to find. I interviewed him at length, and far from being fed up with being interviewed about his mother, as I had expected, he seemed to love it. Rieff turned out to be a flamboyant, amusing interview, and I got enough for a whole article out of him, almost none of which, alas, I had the space to use. I was, however, able to use the things he said to inform my questions and to provoke that delicious moment when Rieff told me that he had stopped calling Sontag "Mommy" at a "preposterously early age," and she said, "That's not true!"

Most of Sontag's friends and acquaintances were far too circumspect to give me anything but the most general of comments—further evidence for my lead. Among others I called Frances Fitzgerald, who said that she didn't really know Sontag. I tried a well-known writer who had once interviewed her years ago, and she intimated that Sontag didn't care for friendships with women but wanted that rather inaccurate comment kept off the record. And I tried Sharon DeLano, an old and close friend of Sontag's, who spoke fondly of her and made fun of her clothes. I also telephoned a couple of Sontag's critics, academics who had written searing satires of her, but none returned my calls. In the end, I had to use quotations from reviews and articles to stand in for her critics, and off-the-record gossip to inform my analyses and questions, but I had learned that Sontag inspired not only fear but hostility in people, especially in academics. In a *Harper's* magazine piece called "Susie Creamcheese Makes Love Not War," for instance, English professor Marvin Mudrick wrote, "Susan Sontag, refusing to settle for English, writes a sort of demotic culturese. . . ." The moral: every interview teaches you something, even if you never use a word of it in print.

The day of the first interview arrived at last, and I landed on Sontag's doorstep nervous and hot. I had seen her in public twice, at readings, but never met her face to face, and felt conscious as every reporter does of the salesmanlike role of coming to a stranger's house to get everything you can out of her.

She let me in with a cautious smile, leading me up the steps to her duplex in the top two floors of the house. I noticed right away that she walked heavily, as if it were costing her effort, and that she looked tired. She was wearing purple and black, a dark combination for a hot summer day and one that she hardly varied the times I saw her.

Her apartment struck me immediately as beautiful. Very white and light, with a red-tiled patio on which potted trees waved in the breeze. She kept me to the public rooms—the kitchen, in which she puttered about making an endless cup of coffee, and the patio, where we were to sit. I peeked into the living room, big and empty, lined with bookshelves and prints, but could only guess about the upstairs, where she said she had her study and bedroom. As if reading my thoughts, she admonished me not to write another silly piece about "all the books" she has. I remembered to keep that particular note of awe out of my article—after all, what would one expect from an author?

We made awkward conversation while she brewed her espresso and my tea, awkward because I didn't want to ask any important questions until my tape was on. Nevertheless, we had a gossip about Joseph Brodsky, with whom she is good friends, and about the notorious Town Hall meeting where she and Brodsky had appeared in support of the Polish Solidarity movement (I opened my Brodsky profile with a description of that scene, and she had read it). Brodsky had thought the entire affair a joke, Sontag said, and had invited her along to "make a ruckus." "So off we went like a couple of naughty kids, and sat backstage for an hour, giggling."

The first moments of meeting someone often make the deepest impressions, and that talk in Sontag's kitchen was no exception. It was there that I discovered that she is both powerfully confident and highly defensive, probably consequences of early success and of being in the public eye for so long. When I suggested that her coffee machine seemed a lot of trouble, for instance, she snapped that, quite the contrary, it was quick. When I admired her apartment and asked if she had rented it for the summer, she said simply, "No! I live here. You don't understand, perhaps because you're not a New Yorker. People don't move in New York. Why should they? This is my home." I was surprised at her irritation, and noticed that it came out especially strongly at any suggestion that she might be rich, an observation I put in the article. On the other hand, she asked me lots of questions about myself and clearly took tremendous delight whenever our opinions concurred. As I wrote in my notes afterwards, "She hates to be misunderstood, but she can be sweet and warm, almost girlishly friendly."

The first interview began slowly and stayed mostly on the subject of AIDS and her books. I sat with my volume of questions on my lap, letting her guide much of the interview in order to feel out where her passions lay. Once in a while I caught myself pretending to listen to her discuss the meaning of words while really thinking, "How on earth am I going to ask her if she dyes that white streak in her hair?" but mostly I concentrated on finding a way to steer her toward the subject of her cancer. I wanted to link her current theories about AIDS (the news peg) with her former brush with death (the human drama), an obvious connection I didn't think she could object to. But by the end of that first interview, I knew I hadn't done it yet. We had spent too much time talking about AIDS and her writing and not enough time talking about Susan Sontag. I made a date for another interview, one month ahead.

Sitting in a nearby restaurant afterward, I jotted down my impressions and went into a mild panic over whether one of the tapes was blank (it wasn't). I recorded my first impression of her combination of irritability and kindness, and noted her smile. "Her smile is a surprise," I wrote. "A very happy, big smile. Big teeth. It changes her face enormously, from sad but elegant to goofy. The bottom half of her face becomes someone else when she smiles. You just don't expect her mouth to make that shape." I used only the essence of these musings in the final piece, but I would have forgotten them altogether had I not recorded them immediately.

In the restaurant I spent almost two hours writing down my impressions of Sontag and relating them to each other and to her work—laying down the first, essential daubs of paint that were to provide the foundation for my portrait.

I had a month between interviews to read more and write a first draft, a luxury I recommend. It enabled me to form theories I knew I could test, to find a shape for the piece, and to pinpoint the holes. It also enabled me to collect more gossip. Sontag is the kind of person about whom people like to speculate endlessly, and even though I had to filter out most of what I'd heard as either prurient or unverifiable, the gossip gave me confidence that I was getting to know my subject.

The second interview was much more relaxed. She was more friendly, as if I had somehow proved myself, and it didn't take long this time to find a more personal tone for the interview. I noticed that she had a rack of underwear drying on her patio, and that, like her clothes, it was all black, but as is the case for many an amusing but trivial detail, I had to leave that out of my piece.

The nearest I got to bringing up Sontag's love life was to ask her why she had married so young, at seventeen. Her answer was a bark: "Oh, but that's like saying how come I've become a writer. How can I answer such a question? I can't vulgarize my own motives and say I was very mature for my age. No, I met someone whom I was drawn to and that seemed the right thing to do. Anything else I would be treating myself as an object." But I didn't lay off her private life out of fear. I decided that the quotations I had from her about death, loneliness, and her need for intimacy were far more dramatic, and more interesting, than the subject of her sex life. By making that decision, however, I had taken a risk, for I knew the editors might force me to call her back and blurt out an awful question such as "Who are you sleeping with and is it true you once had an affair with X?" Rather than confront the editors with my decision on this matter, I decided to give them my piece without comment and hope they would be pleased enough with it to forget about the sex. And that is exactly what happened.

But with the matter of the hair, things were not so simple. Sontag's dramatic streak of white hair is such a part of her look—no cartoonist would leave it out—that I couldn't ignore it. So there I was, near the end of the second interview, knowing I'd won Sontag's respect by asking her serious, intelligent questions, trying to find a way of introducing this silly hair dye business without wrecking the mood. I tiptoed toward the subject by bringing up makeup.

I put the blame on my editors (a useful trick whenever you have to ask trivial, intrusive, or embarrassing questions) and said they wanted me to ask her why she never wore makeup—whether it was a political decision. Sontag gave me a marvelous answer.

"Well, actually, it's because I think I don't need to. I actually feel attractive enough without it!" After a laugh, she went on. "There's nothing political about it. I think it's wonderful that people try to make themselves beautiful. I dye my hair, for instance, and I certainly would not pretend not to." And she went on to explain what I put in the profile, that the streak had been natural until chemotherapy had turned her gray, while I gazed on in gratitude, the relief practically lifting me out of my chair.

But the real breakthrough came when Sontag made the following statement: "I don't want to do much more essay writing. I feel I've had my shot, I've had my run. I could make better use of my talents in writing in a freer, more emotionally direct way." As soon as I heard this, the writerly machine began clicking like mad in my head. Here was someone who had become famous and highly respected for her essays talking about giving them up. Here was a woman generally thought of as coldly intellectual, yearning to write emotionally. I realized instantly, as she spoke, that this tied together all the elements I had been looking for: what I came to call her "move toward the personal." Her wish to write more personally fit in with her passion about AIDS, with her having accepted the presidency of PEN, with the crusading tone of her new book, even with her agreeing to be profiled for a women's magazine. I realized that the public image of Sontag as aloof from life, intimidating and cold was wrong, and probably a result of the sexist stereotyping of an intelligent woman. And I saw, right there on her patio, watching her sip coffee, fiddle with her watch, and shift about on her couch, that I had my theme.

Once I got home with my four hours of interviews—twenty-seven pages of single-spaced transcripts—there began the usual song and dance with editors. They wanted the piece written in ten days, to make the November issue. I wanted four weeks—this was only August. The publishers wanted it postponed until January, because the publication date of the AIDS books had been pushed forward. The magazine wanted it out in November because they wanted a scoop. Scoops are everything in journalism, so, after quite a bit of wrangling, the magazine won, of course, and I wrote the piece in ten days.

My editors were graceful and I lost only two battles, length and tense. I wanted the piece to be in past tense because it seemed to suit my tone, but in this era of television, present tense is in. And I had to cut out two favorite quotations, a lot about her childhood, and some amusing stuff from David Rieff so the piece could fit in the magazine's "well," jargon for the space between advertisements. (I have restored some of this lost material in the version reprinted here.)

The reaction? The predictable silence. I saw David Rieff at a public event; he grinned at me, shrugged, and loped off without a word. I called the publicist, who assured me that Sontag and everyone else was pleased. Three months later I heard from Sontag, who said she hadn't responded earlier because she is always "embarrassed by these things," but that she found the piece "warm" and thought it captured the flavor of our conversation. And myself, the consummate critic? As every writer says, there is a better version lying in my desk at home, the version that advertising space and publication dates never allowed to live.

TWO

Flight from Predictability

■

PHOTOGRAPH © 1987, BENGT JANGFELDT.

JOSEPH BRODSKY

And when they would finally arrest me for espionage,
for subversive activity, vagrancy, for *ménage*
      à trois, and the crowd, boiling around me, would bellow,
poking me with their work-roughened forefingers, "Outsider!
                    We'll settle your hash!"—
then I would secretly smile, and say to myself, "See,
this your chance to find out, in Act Three,
      how it looks from the inside—you've stared long enough
                        at the outside—
so take note of every detail as you shout, *'Vive la Patrie!'* "[1]

■

Joseph Brodsky looked out of place. He was sitting, impatiently fiddling and yawning, on the stage of New York City's Town Hall with a host of other venerable writers and activists as part of a protest against Poland's martial law. The organizers, "American Workers and Artists for Solidarity," had invited him because he is an exiled Russian poet of the highest standing and vociferously anti-Soviet. If they had expected him to stand up with them as a fellow leftist, however, they were wrong.

On stage with him were Susan Sontag, E. L. Doctorow, Kurt Vonnegut, Allen Ginsberg, Paul Robeson, Jr., Pete Seeger, and others, but Brodsky sat apart from them, staring gloomily at the floor. His face, pink, smooth, and round, glistened under the lights, his thinning amber hair was sticky with sweat, and his crumpled brown suit and blue shirt stretched across his plump stomach. He had on a little, rather comic bow tie, and he smoked and frowned a lot.

For three hours, the liberal and leftist audience was regaled with causes: Reagan's unsympathetic treatment of the air traffic controllers' strike, El Salvador, Nicaragua, Iran—all were related in some way to Poland's martial law. Sontag quoted Brodsky in her speech ("Banks, not tanks, did Poland in"), and then made her by now renowned statement, "Communism is fascism with a human face," a phrase that reverberated through the nation for weeks. After she left the stage in a cloud of boos and cheers, Pete Seeger loped up to the microphone. "Long live controversy!" he shouted. Brodsky clapped.

When it was at last Brodsky's turn to speak, he walked up to the podium looking small, creased, and annoyed. He began by "umming" and "ahhing" a lot, which made the audience tense; then, speaking in quick, angry bursts, he said, "You liberals in search of a cause should apply pressure to Washington. Write to your congressman and demand that we withdraw U.S. troops from West Germany. This will sober up the Germans and make them invest in other places than Eastern Europe. This is much more effective than organizing trade unions here." The audience stirred uneasily and some people hissed, but Brodsky was not to be stopped. He grew angrier.

"Not only is drawing a parallel from PATCO to the Polish workers an outright obscenity," he said in reference to a previous speaker, "it distracts people from the real issues and leaves Poland out in the cold where it is already. You liberals should try to solve one problem instead of diffusing your energy all over the world!"

The audience erupted into boos. One enraged man sprang to his feet and shouted, "You cynical bastard!"

Brodsky is used to infuriating people. In his native Soviet Union, he confounded authorities with his contradictions—a Jew indifferent to Judaism, a critic of communism who called himself a "neutralist," a writer of poetry that was intensely personal and yet uncomfortably political. Unable to prove him an active dissident, Soviet authorities had to resort to accusations of "decadent," "corruptor of youth," and "pornographer" to get Brodsky into jail and eventually out of their country. Now, just because he has been welcomed in America, showered with awards, and hailed, at only forty-three, as the best living Russian poet, he is not about to stop ruffling tempers.

Two weeks after the Solidarity meeting, I went to see Brodsky in his quiet basement apartment in Greenwich Village. I had to track him down by mail because he teaches in Michigan and is constantly en route, but he responded quickly with a postcard pointedly titled "Kiss of the Muse."

"I have nothing against an interview except for a normal set of reservations every writer has about prattling instead of writing," he wrote in a jagged black scrawl. "Still, I should think I'll be able to overcome that."

Brodsky greeted me with polite coolness and ushered me into his dark living room. He was wearing a red plaid shirt under a black vest and looked taller and younger than he had on stage. "I have only instant coffee or Campari, so I suppose it's coffee?" he said, his accent still thickly Russian, with guttural consonants and lilting vowels.

"Do you mind a tape recorder?" I asked.

"I mind nothing." He shrugged and spoke in a tone of indifference, as if all but the worst tortures would only make him yawn. I told him I'd been at the Solidarity meeting and had heard the audience's boos.

"The hooting I don't care very much about," he answered, "but I regret I could not speak for longer. The guys there deserved a lot more whipping for the thing." Apparently forgetting about the coffee, he took a seat in a chair opposite me. "American liberal thinking is astonishingly provincial. To find yourself in 1982 listening to all those ravings, all that lingo of socialists, of communists, of sympathizers—it's unseemly. Stupidly enough, I still care about what people think, and I simply don't like them to be manipulated by wits that I consider dimmer than mine."

He chuckled and patted his pockets for cigarettes, looking not the least apologetic for this arrogant statement. "Where are my . . . ?" He lifted my notebook off the coffee table, espied his packet of Kents underneath it, and looked at me in mock accusation. Brodsky had heart bypass surgery four years ago and he is not supposed to smoke. He took out a cigarette, bit down on the filter, yanked it out with his teeth, and threw it into the fireplace.

Brodsky's rise to fame in this country was astonishingly quick. He arrived here eleven years ago, a stunned émigré who had only a rough mastery of English. (He had taught himself in Russia by painstakingly translating the first and last verses of English poems with the use of a dictionary, and then writing the middles as he thought, poetically, they should read.) Since then he has become what the *New York Times* called "a fixture in our literary landscape." His poetry is now published in all the prestigious magazines, his two books of translated verse, *Selected Poems* and *A Part of Speech*, moved reviewers to extravagant praise, and he has never been short of teaching positions.* But he lives humbly. Poets do not get rich. His one-bedroom apartment is simple and cold, the unpolished wooden floor is bare, the fireplace for now dead, and the only decorations postcards, posters, and books. The one piece

---

* Since this writing, Brodsky also won the 1987 Nobel Prize for Literature.

of magnificence is his desk, a huge, gleaming antique resplendent with curls and cubbyholes and smothered in photographs. Next to it, on the floor, is a thigh-high red and white Coca-Cola can—his wastepaper basket.

Brodsky went into his tiny kitchen, really nothing but a stove in a hallway, to make the coffee. I asked him what he thought of Sontag's statement equating communism with fascism.

"I agree with Susan," he said, carrying the mugs over to the table. "I think she just opened the box a little. To me, the difference between communism and fascism is that the latter lost the war."

"What do you mean?"

"I would have thought that was self-evident." He put the coffee down. "Let me explain it. We've all been brought up within a certain mythological framework—that is, we're used to regarding every struggle as a battle between good and bad, demon and angel. The last war was simply a struggle between two demons. Fascism and communism were equal partners in that battle, in a sense, brothers. It was a battle between two demons and one demon lost. In Eastern Europe, where I, in a sense, come from, this sense that communism is not any different from fascism is a very old idea. Even as schoolboys we were struck with the structural similarity of both—the same authoritarian setup, a system whose purpose is subjugation of an individual."

"But why are you so annoyed at American liberals?" I asked.

"Because this has been known for forty years. It's simply annoying to see in the West still an argument being made that one thing is better than another."

I asked him why he suggested the United States threaten to withdraw its troops from West Germany.

"Not only West Germany, other European countries, too. Because this would make the West European bankers think at least twice before they would give further credits to the Eastern block. Maybe they would invest more here instead! I also think, by the way, that the gas pipeline deal that the Germans and French advocate so vigorously could be simply regarded as a benevolent version of the Final Solution—that the Europeans are going to be gassed by the Soviets. I don't see any reason why the Soviet Union wouldn't introduce a poison into that pipeline!" He laughed.

Brodsky's antipathy to communism comes, of course, from personal experience, and since he has been here, he has actively opposed it. He frequently signs petitions protesting the same kind of persecution of artists that he went through, and he also helps newly defected Russians whenever he can. When the ballet dancer Alexander Gudenov defected, for example, Brodsky interpreted and negotiated for him and took him around New York.

Brodsky's own persecution began in his early twenties. His poetry was never officially accepted by Soviet authorities, perhaps because of its bleak, subtly critical tone (which Brodsky says was nothing but the normal melancholia of youth); so he could publish it only illegally in underground journals. He also helped other unapproved writers distribute their work. These activities got Brodsky arrested and thrown into jail on several occasions ("a terribly hungry time"). Then, when he was twenty-four, he was convicted of "social parasitism" and sentenced to five years' hard labor in a remote corner of northern Russia.

"By this they meant I was a drifter," he explained. "I was accused of changing thirteen jobs within six years, and no society likes that sort of thing. I read the list of accusations against me— there were about sixteen. All the terminology of persecution was there." Before he was exiled, however, he was put through an even worse punishment: he was sent twice to a mental institution.

"There they do to you things really quite painful and scary," he told me, leaning forward to pick up my leftover coffee. He poured it into his mug and drank. "They give you all sorts of injections that make you scream with pain when you move. They get you out of bed in the middle of the night, wrap you in bedsheets, and plunge you in the cold water bath, and you don't know whether they are going to stop. You heard about that, but still, when it happens to your body, it's sort of a novelty." He shrugged and looked up with a direct flash of his pale blue eyes. He seemed embarrassed by what he was saying, a man who does not like to admit to suffering.

"It's pretty terrifying," he continued. "They fish you out and leave you wrapped up in that sheet and the sheet starts to dry up and it gets into your skin, and it's terribly painful. And they beat you up. But the main thing is you watch yourself. When you cross the threshold they tell you that the first sign of good mental health is sound sleep, and you lie in your bed and you can't sleep. You think that maybe you are really going insane." He rocked back in his chair, decapitated another cigarette, and chuckled, as if he had just told a joke.

"Didn't you hate the people who were doing those things to you?" I asked.

"Not really. I knew that they're the masters and I'm just me. People who do nasty things deserve pity. But I was young, you see, so I was fairly careless. At that time I had on my hands the first and last major triangle in my life. A *ménage à trois*—the usual thing, two men and a woman—and therefore my mind was occupied mostly by that. What happens in your mind is much more disturbing than what happens to your body."

Just then, the phone rang. Brodsky eagerly picked it up—a way out of this painful conversation. After greeting his friend happily, he said, "I must tell you right at the beginning that I read your translations and the poems are worthless." The friend clearly responded with gloom, for Brodsky then said, "It's better to assume shit than roses, yuh?" Later, by way of comfort, he added, "But you know it's a sin to despair."

While Brodsky was on the phone, I watched him, thinking he would not be an easy friend to have. Loyal, but brutal if he felt like it. The love of truth he expresses in his poetry can, I saw, be exercised at the expense of tact. On the phone, he was alternately funny and kind, conceited and cruel; and former students of his told me that although he can be wonderful if he likes your work, he can otherwise be devastating. Brodsky is an odd combination of arrogance and timidity, a man whose shyness can sometimes seem like contempt. This impression is partly the fault of his trouble with English—his speech is constantly interrupted by long strings of "ums" as he searches for words—but he is shy and he is private. When I asked him how his health is, for example, he looked away from me and shrugged in embarrassment. "Well, I don't really know," he said reluctantly, and giggled. "Precarious. Well, I wish I were healthier, it's as simple as that, because it gets in my way more." Lately Brodsky's poems have been dwelling on age and mortality:

> My life has dragged on. The signs are plenty.
> They'd make yet another life, just as dragging. . . .
>
> My life had dragged on. One cold resembles another
> cold. Time looks like time. . . .[2]

"I used to think that there is some sort of link between me and my students on the basis of age," he told me after the phone call, "but this February, I walked in the classroom and saw their faces, which are terribly young, and I realized this is real teaching now. We are talking from opposite ends of life." He paused, looking bemused.

"My feeling was that until the age of thirty-three or -four, I remembered my life in great detail. I was able to recall on which side of an open book I read this or that sentence. Presently, I seldom remember what happened in the morning." He laughed. "It's quite puzzling, but then, no matter what's happening to me, it's truth."

After Brodsky's stints in the mental institutions were over, he was sent to work on a community farm in Arkhangelsk, a remote area of Russia near the Arctic Circle. There he moved boulders, shepherded, reaped, and sowed, and he says he did not mind this existence at all. The punishment was, for him, a poetic experience, a fact he considers quite a joke on the Soviet government.

"The rural community there is so bleak, the only thing you have at your disposal is the bottle, which we called the Cossak TV," he told me. "The villages are impoverished, people never see meat. The only thing in the stores is bottles of vodka, like the collected works of Dickens on a shelf. Every shelf is covered.

"But the farm where I lived was quite nice. It was God knows where, among the bogs, but I had a very nice wooden hut. It was terribly old-fashioned, like in the novels, or like better still, Robert Frost. I loved it."

During this time, Brodsky taught himself English and wrote poetry. He says it was one of his most prolific periods. "You see, in agriculture, there are days, especially in winter, when you can't do much. So your write, yuh?"

> Buried alive here,
> I wade through twilight stubble. . . .
>
> My frozen hand pressed to my hips,
> I roam from mound to hillock—
> without memories, with only an inner noise:
> I bend down over a dark stream,
> and recoil in shock.
>
> but is this a face, or the scene
> of a landslide?
>
> It's as though I'm not really here,
> but somewhere on the sidelines, somewhere overboard.[3]

The poems Brodsky wrote during this exile reveal a suffering he won't admit to in conversation. They are sad and bleak, set in stark landscapes where he is so alone that tiny movements become avalanches and sounds explosions:

> the buzzing of a blindingly bright wasp
> above a simple daisy can unnerve me.[4]

They also express sharp longings:

> But a caress remote from loving arms,
> when miles take you aback, stabs at your brain
> harder than kisses: separation's sky
> is solider than any ceilinged shelter.[5]

When I asked him if having been wrenched from family, lovers, and friends made him lonely, however, he denied it. "Perhaps I am to some degree a misanthrope," he said offhandedly. "I missed maybe two or three people, but you always miss two or three people, don't you?

"And then there were the villagers—not terribly well educated or bright, but I got along with them well. In fact, when I was leaving, some of them, myself included, we were crying. Poets are born democrats, you see. Unlike prose writers, they don't need much for their operation. It's like a bird, it will sing on any branch it perches, yuh? It somehow assumes that somebody's listening to it.

"Besides," he continued, "I liked the language the villagers spoke. There were a great deal of old words. I remember one day, I walked into the house and an old woman, a terribly old hag, stood in front of the window and there was a blizzard going on." He stopped speaking and smiled wistfully, as if giving up all hope of being understood. "I can't refer to it in English because it doesn't translate. . . ." he paused again. "Well, she used the word for blizzard and I was terribly moved. Because you don't hear that word now, you see?"

The sensitivity to language that helped nurse Brodsky through his exile on the farm is largely what led him to write poetry in the first place, although writing was also his way of defying an oppressive regime. ("I was raised by a cold that, to warm my palm / gathered my fingers around a pen," he has written in a poem.)[6] He began writing poetry at eighteen.

"What really started me writing poetry is a certain notion of harmony, of sound, I used to say a certain hum that you have in your head," he said. "The hum is the voice of the language. Popularly they call it the voice of the muse, but it's simply the language —what you've read, what you've heard. Writing poetry is simply a terrific acceleration for one's mental operations, yuh? And this is what hooks you."

Now that Brodsky lives in America, his poetry can rarely be read or recited in its original language, but Brodsky still writes most of it in Russian first anyway. "I write for a kind of angel of the Russian language," he joked. He publishes these versions in European and émigré magazines that are sometimes smuggled into the Soviet Union, but eventually he must translate. Lately, he has been doing this more and more himself.

"It's not because I don't trust other people," he said, "but merely because it hurts very much when you see a version that is simply in bad English. I try to talk to the translator, but this results in offending people. After all, everybody has an ego.

"But it's maddening to translate. It's trying to keep as much as you can of the original in English, but naturally enough you cannot, yuh? And I resent this."

> denied a chalice at the feast of the fatherland,
> now I stand in a strange place. The name hardly matters. . . .

> here I'll live out my days, losing gradually
> hair, teeth, consonants, verbs, and suffixes. . . .[7]

Brodsky told me he now speaks Russian one-third to one-half as much as he did at home, with friends or just to himself.

"Are you losing the 'melody' of your language?" I asked.

He looked over my head and shoved his hands down the neck of his shirt for warmth. "I think it's getting dimmer, yes," he said slowly, "but it's a form of truth that it's getting dimmer, and I try to fit into that. You realize that you and your language are locked in a *tête à tête* situation."

In fact, Brodsky's divorce from his language troubles him quite a bit, as I found out when I went to hear him give a reading to a small college audience in New York. As at the Solidarity meeting, he was at first nervous, fiddling with things on the podium, "umming" and "ahhing," trying to drink water out of an empty glass. He began by reading some poems in English, including one about the Soviet invasion of Afghanistan, but he read too fast and made too many mispronunciations for the audience to be able to understand him. Every now and then, in a gesture of impatience or despair, he broke off in midsentence, ran his hand over his balding head, and said, "This is simply tiresome in English."

Then, at the end, he recited a poem in Russian. It was not one of his, but one by Marina Tsvetaeva, whom he admires, and he knew it by heart. He lifted up his head, his face suddenly cleared of lines as if ten years had been smoothed away by an invisible caress, and he chanted the poem in the Russian manner, his voice swelling to a dramatic crescendo. The effect, even to one who can't understand Russian, was deeply moving. I realized then that Brodsky still strains over our language. His face is constantly knotted with effort.

> And a nameless lodger, a nobody, boards the boat,
> a bottle of grappa concealed in his raincoat
>   as he gains his shadowy room, bereaved
> of memory, homeland, son, with only the noise
> of distant forests to grieve for his former joys,
>   if anyone is grieved.[8]

After serving less than half his sentence on the farm, Brodsky was suddenly released and allowed to return to Leningrad. (He was released the year after Brezhnev came into power, and his release was announced on the same day as the decree for the arrests of two other writers, Andrei Sinyavsky and Yuli Daniel. "So the sacred spot is never empty," Brodsky said sardonically.) But then, seven years later, he was summoned suddenly to the Ministry of Interior and commanded to leave the country forever. On June 4, 1972, he was put on a plane to Vienna, never to return. Once again, he had been yanked away from his life, his friends, and his family, including this time a son born out of wedlock.

"My parents are fairly old, in their late seventies, and I'm their only child. I've been trying to invite them all these ten years, but they've been systematically turned down," he told me. "The authorities simply replied that 'we don't find this visit purposeful.' This is the kind of country it is."

> And as for where in space and time one's toe end touches,
> well, earth is hard all over; try the States.[9]

When Brodsky landed in Vienna, he was met by a friend who whisked him off to the United States to teach at the University of

Michigan. He has been teaching ever since, likes it, and plans to continue. He also plans to keep living here rather than in Europe, partly, he says, because he liked American poetry.

"A nation is lucky when it has two or three great poets in a century," he told me, "and America had Robert Frost and Robert Lowell, as well as Wallace Stevens. It is interesting for me to read modern American poetry because sometimes you see a terribly whimsical mind in operation. The quality of perception is high, and that is perhaps the only thing that interests me in poetry.

"But American poetry does suffer a malaise of form. These people cannot master either traditional or new forms, and therefore it is not going to survive. One of the purposes of poetry is to create an air of inevitability of what's being said. This is what you have form for, yuh? So that you cannot really erase it from your mind. I don't remember who said this, but it's only through form that the work of the mind can be elevated above commonplace."

During his years here, Brodsky has come to be embraced by the poetry world. His poems have been translated into at least ten languages and he has received the MacArthur Foundation award. Nevertheless, as for all poets in this country, the audiences at his readings are usually small, the print runs of his books tiny, and his pay modest. In Russia, on the other hand, an officially accepted poet of his standing here would be treated with reverence. People of all types would turn out by the hundreds for readings, celebratory candles would be lit, flowers strewn at his feet. I asked Brodsky if he ever longs for this sort of glory. He frowned at the question, then helped himself to the rest of my coffee.

"People are thirsty for literature in Russia, but what they get is the state approved substitute for it," he said severely. "They are in a sense deceived. Besides, there is a difference between a centralized state and democracy! I prefer oblivion in democracy to being *la crème de la crème* in a tyranny.

"Quite a lot of Russians are happy living a very minimal existence here merely because they are happy that they don't have to lie or listen to lies."

"But we do have to listen to lies," I said, thinking of Vietnam and, more recently, El Salvador. "Isn't that a rather romantic view of America?"

"I wouldn't say so," Brodsky replied. "If anything, that romance is justified. Even though the government may lie, there are quite a lot of sources to learn the truth from. Journalists will try to do everything in their power to undo that lie, whereas in Russia you don't have this."

Brodsky has despised the "tryanny" of the Soviet government almost all his life. He minded it and felt it intimately even when he was very young, for to him, a totalitarian state is not just oppressive politics but a condition that stifles the soul. In his memoir of growing up in Leningrad, "Less Than One" (part of a book of essays of the same title) he describes how he hated the dull, blunt architecture that the Soviets erected in place of old buildings; the same blue line that ran around the rooms of schools, factories, and prisons alike; the picture of Lenin that glared down on him from endless walls.

At fifteen, already exasperated by repetition and dullness, he walked out of school, never to return. "I simply couldn't stand certain faces in my class—of some of my classmates, but mostly of teachers. . . . Of the emotions overpowering me at the moment, I remember only a general disgust with myself for being too young and for letting so many things boss me around."

He now regards leaving school as his first "free act." "It was an instinctive act, a walkout," he wrote. "Reason had very little to do with it. I know that, because I've been walking out ever since, with increasing frequency." It is this attitude that leads him to infuriate people—the Soviet authorities, the American Left, and also Western Jews, who have objected to Brodsky because he refuses to embrace ethnic identification and uses a great deal of Christian imagery in his poems.

"I have not exactly been manhandled, but I've had my cup to drink with Jews since I came to the West, and I resent this," Brodsky told me. "Westerners can't really swallow properly that in Russia, Christianity and Judaism are not divorced that much. In Russia we regard the New Testament as a spin-off of the Old. Whatever happened to Jesus is somehow prefigured by the prophets. In a sense, we are more scholars of both testaments than worshipers—or, at least, I am."

I had heard a rumor that, since coming to the West, Brodsky had converted to Christianity. I asked him if this was true.

"That is stark, raving nonsense!" he said sharply. "I haven't got time." He laughed and looked at me slyly. "I'm a bad Jew." Then he got more serious. "I think one should identify oneself in a more precise fashion than race or creed or nationality. One should first figure out whether one is a coward, or an honest or dishonest man. One's identity shouldn't depend on outer criteria."

Brodsky's rejection of rules, labels, systems—his perpetual walking out—has held true for his personal life as well. He lives alone, has never married.

"What about love?" I asked. "Are you walking away from that, too?"

He picked up a little toy lion that was, for some reason, sitting on the coffee table and began to twist its mane in his fingers.

"Well, that falls in the same category, yuh," he said at last. "It's simply that of all those things we are told matter most—love, work, et cetera—only work survives. And if you are doing work seriously, your choice is between life, that is love, and work. You realize that you can't master both. You have to fake one, so you fake life. In more particular terms, you realize that you regard your beloved as kind of a part-time thing, whereas your work is full time. But she regards love as full time, and there's the rub. Also, in itself, work is walking way from yourself."

"But why the need to keep walking away?"

Brodsky put down the lion, which by now looked like a Rastafarian. "It's a flight from predictability," he replied. "It becomes less and less possible to settle for a certain notion, for any form of mental or existential routine." He covered his face with his hands wearily, and rubbed long and hard.

"Largely it has to do with that desperate sense of being *no one* that, I must say, is fairly peculiar to my humble self. I have always in one way or another sensed it. You are more or less life's or death's, but not anything or anyone else's." He looked up and smiled slightly. "You are unclaimed."

BRODSKY COMMENTARY

T he profile of Joseph Brodsky, and some of the others in this book, originally came about because of an old trick in journalism commonly known as "cultivating sources." I had come to know the head of the publicity department at Farrar, Straus, and Giroux, the book publisher that has more Nobel laureates on its list than any other in the country, and we would talk occasionally about who was coming out with a new book. This gave my source a chance to seek some publicity for her writers and gave me a chance to find a news peg, or excuse, for profiling some of my favorite authors. In this way I discovered that Brodsky's first book of prose, *Less Than One*, was due to be published in a few months. (The book was eventually postponed until 1986.)

Armed with this information, I approached *Esquire* magazine, having noticed that it had recently run a long profile of Saul Bellow and seemed interested in the literati all of a sudden. Although the magazine normally featured basketball players, actresses, or racing car drivers, not poets, much to my (and later Brodsky's) surprise, an editor agreed to assign me the story. She gave me four weeks to write it in, and four thousand words, a length that proved both a blessing and a curse.

With *Esquire* backing me, it was not hard to approach Brodsky. True, he was already being recognized as *the* poet of the times, although he was not yet a Nobel laureate, but it turned out that Brodsky had once been given a subscription to *Esquire* and rather enjoyed it; so he agreed, and the date was set.

I prepared by going to see him speak with Susan Sontag and others at the Town Hall meeting and by reading his two translated books of poetry and all the interviews with him I could find. At first I was daunted. His poems are not easily accessible to the lay public, and his essays are often dense with allusions and political ideas. But as I studied them, I noticed a recurring theme of him as an exile from his own language, a particularly ironic, painful predicament for a poet. I wanted to delve deeper into that theme than other journalists had and also to portray him and his past more fully. What is more, when I read his poetry side by side with his interviews and essays, and thought over his defiant and irritated appearance at the Solidarity meeting, I began to see emotion and a thread of autobiography behind his intellectual language. Nevertheless, when the day of the interview arrived, I could not shake my trepidation. I was afraid, simply, that I had not understood what I'd read.

I arrived at his home in Greenwich Village, a pretty red-brick town house on Morton Street, and found a note pinned on the door saying, "The bell now working." I rang the doorbell, was buzzed in, and stepped into a long, dark hallway where I stood, confused, listening to a voice emanating from the house's depths. "Hello?" it shouted.

"Hello? Which way do I go?" I called back rather lamely.

"Downstairs," came the somber reply.

He was waiting in the dark hall by his open door, with a weary and bored expression on his face. He welcomed me without a smile and without much enthusiasm.

My first impression was of a depressing darkness. His one-bedroom, railroad apartment was in the basement, and not only lacked light but looked as dimmed with age as some Dickensian antechamber. The floors were dark wood, in need of a polish, there were no rugs, and the tiny, diamond-shaped panes of the window blocked out most of the little light there might have been. The apartment looked as if Brodsky were temporarily inhabiting it, like a college student—there were even postcards plastered all over the inside of the door. A poster of an Oleg Tselkov sculpture, a red face with black holes for eyes and mouth, stared out at me. The effect was sinister.

Brodsky himself, as I said in the piece, looked younger and more attractive than he had on the Town Hall stage. I was particularly struck by his golden-red hair, which, though thinning, caught the light in beautiful gleams, and his disconcertingly pale blue eyes, rimmed by glinting red-gold eyelashes. His sculptured nose and thin lips looked ready to curl with disdain at any moment.

He showed me to a large, hairy brown sofa in his living room—study and sat in a rocking chair next to the dead-looking fireplace. Right away I knew he wasn't going to lift a finger to make this interview easy for me. I was going to have to struggle to get anything personal out of him, and I was going to be watched sardonically the whole time I did it. He seemed ready to pounce on any sign of ignorance or idiocy.

Sometimes, in an interview, I can find a common ground with my subject that helps us both to relax. It might be age, interests, gender, common experience or opinion, or simply a confluence of personalities. I did not sense this with Brodsky. He seemed to regard me as very young and as attached to a frivolous magazine —although I knew a lot about him, he knew nothing about me. I sensed that he was not inclined to take me seriously, so I had to prolong the interview as long as I could. In a sense, I had to question him until, exhausted, his defenses broke down. I sat there relentlessly for two and a half hours, questioning him, listening in on his phone calls, glued to that couch. When I transcribed the tape afterward, I had over forty single-spaced pages of quotations.

He talked politics, Russia, history, poetry, Europe, America, immigration, opinions. He told me about the Soviet economic and agricultural systems, about the plight of modern-day poetry, about facism and the Soviet pipelines. And in between all this, he let out, bit by bit and most reluctantly, information about his own life. Whenever I asked him about his health, or his treatment in jail and mental institutions, he squirmed, looked away from me, and answered briefly. And when I tried, for the sake of *Esquire*, to ask him about his personal life—his *"menage à trois,"* his illegitimate son —he was sharp and off-putting.

BENEDICT: Was the triangle you mentioned to me the same as the *menage à trois* you had in your poem?

BRODSKY: More or less.

BENEDICT: You and two women?

BRODSKY: No no no. It was the usual thing. One woman, two men. But I'd rather be less precise about that.

BENEDICT (taking deep breath): Are you not in correspondence with your son for political or personal reasons? (Here is the interviewer giving the interviewee an escape hatch, out of embarrassment. I should have asked, "Why aren't you in touch with your son?")

BRODSKY: This is none of *Esquire*'s business. For your own consumption, it's more the latter. Well, it's actually a neat balance of the two. But do explain to *Esquire* that all those concerns pale in comparison to the search for a good sentence or a good line.

It wasn't until the very end of the interview, when we were both becoming reckless with exhaustion, and I was able to ask him directly about love. And his answer, his description of walking away from things all his life, including love, gave me my theme then and there on his hairy couch. I saw his defiance in the Town Hall, the rebelliousness of his childhood, his statements about Jews and liberals, and his love life all fitting together into that "flight from predictability," the phrase that became the title and backbone of my piece.

When I ended the interview, dizzy from listening and concentrating, he, too, looked drained. I said, "Okay, I will now leave you in peace"; he replied, "Yuh, have mercy. I didn't know I knew so many words."

In a nearby bagel restaurant, I immediately scribbled down four pages of description. Brodsky had displayed several quirky, and I thought revealing, mannerisms. He tore off cigarette filters with his teeth, in spite of having been told to give up smoking by his doctors, suggesting either a death wish or extraordinary macho rebelliousness (more likely the latter, I came to conclude). He swiveled in his chair to toss his ashes into the fireplace rather than using the ashtray right in front of him, a habit I guessed had stemmed from more primitive living. He crossed his wrists and stuffed his hands down the neck of his shirt, making himself look small and defensive. He helped himself, twice, to my coffee, without asking, perhaps indicating a frugality born of earlier days of hunger and privation. He fiddled with his toy lion when he felt cornered, revealing a touchingly childlike anxiety. And he rubbed his face long and hard as he began to tire toward the end of the interview, showing an unselfconsciousness that comes, perhaps, with confidence.

His room, too, was revealing. I have spoken of the contrast between his elaborate Victorian desk and the giant Coca-Cola wastepaper basket. But I also thought that his lack of concern for luxury, fashion, or even comfort in his furnishing indicated his indifference to his material surroundings—an indifference he displayed again when he refused to complain about his living conditions in exile. And the temporary look of the posters and postcards decorating his room suggested that he had learned not to get too attached to any one place. These were all clues to the inner Brodsky, and although I couldn't interpret them too freely in print, my interpretations being only conjectures, I could certainly present them to the reader as they had been presented to me.

As I went over my notes and his poetry again, I found that his poems and the interview began to fit and support one another. Where he had been unwilling to reveal sadness, his poetry did it for him. Where his poetry was obscure, some of his quotations filled me in on the facts. Not that his poetry is all autobiographical, but it did help me sew together a picture of his inner as well as his outer life.

But I had not really understood the tragedy of Brodsky's position as an exile from his own medium until I went to see him read in Russian, some time after our interview. I was so struck by his transformation when he spoke his own language—his face relaxed, he seemed to grow taller and younger and gentler—that I realized a great deal of what I'd taken as arrogance was really anxiety and frustration. Brodsky does speak English well, but his accent is thick, and the language clearly is, or was at the time, still a struggle for him. That reading turned out to be essential to the tone of my piece, for it enabled me to see Brodsky in a somewhat poignant light, which gave me the chance to reach for a new depth and sympathy in my descriptions of him. This discovery illustrates why it is essential to see a profile subject in different contexts, for even a long, intimate, one-on-one interview reveals only a corner of a soul.

The struggle to whittle down forty pages of interview into an article, even a long one, was difficult, and took me six weeks. I had to leave out one of my favorite quotations, for instance, about sex and art. I had asked him if the Russians were as obsessed with psychology as Americans, and this had led to a discussion of Freud and his theory that creativity is a sublimation of the sexual urge.

"I'm not so sure what is the sublimation of what," Brodsky said. "It may be the reverse—that sexual activity is the sublimation of one's creative urge. In a sense we all know that promiscuity is fairly creative, that the person who is engaged in it is capable of coming up with lies heretofore unknown, you know? But," he continued, "the genres of sexual activity are quite limited. It's like a cow, you can squeeze only two gallons of milk, or whatever it is. You can do this, this, and this, and then comes the ceiling. Whereas with art, you can go on and on!" Brodsky laughed.

I also had to leave out the gossip I'd heard from former students of his and from people who knew him in the publishing and literary party circuit about his friendships with Mikhail Baryshnikov (to whom his untitled classical ballet poem was dedicated) and the poet Derek Walcott, and the way they went out together to drink and pick up women. Brodsky, I'd heard, had a wild side to him, but as he hadn't revealed it to me in person, and as these stories weren't substantiated, I couldn't put them in my piece.

Esquire asked for a rewrite. My editor, who has since left—an intelligent, literate, and sensitive woman who was one of the few female editors on the magazine—confided to me that the "bear den" of editors wanted more "virile and muscular" prose. I toyed with the idea of sending back the piece with little biceps sketched all over it, but I rewrote, going after not virility but coherence, and *Esquire* bought the piece.

Eighteen months later, the profile still had not been published. I telephoned to find out why, and was told that Phillip Moffitt, the magazine's then editor and president, had gone out to dinner with Brodsky, formed his own impressions about him, and wanted me to rewrite the piece incorporating them. I refused. I had written the piece to my satisfaction, had it accepted, and had it paid for. I did not want to compromise my portrait of Brodsky by trying to insert someone else's, and wasn't sure I'd be able to if I tried. In other words, the portrait painter in me balked. I withdrew the piece and published it in the *Antioch Review*. Decently, *Esquire* allowed me to keep my fee.

Brodsky gave me the usual grimace and shrug about the piece when I met him at a party, muttering about how reading a portrait of oneself is never pleasant, but the profile remains one of my favorites. The length I was allowed, the gentle and intelligent editing I received from Marilyn Johnson, the *Esquire* editor, and the six weeks to write and rewrite paid off. What is more, the piece won me Sontag's approval and permission to interview her. Thus, as is often true in journalism, one piece led to another.

THREE

Undaunted and
Undefeated

■

PHOTOGRAPH BY MARTHA SWOPE ASSOCIATES, CAROL ROSEGG.

BEVERLY SILLS

I once walked on the beach with Mrs. Kennedy. It was after both her boys had been murdered, and I said to her, "I just don't know how you've stood what you have." And she said, "Well, I think that sometimes God inflicts the most suffering on the people he loves the most. And every once in a while, I clench my fist and I shake it up to heaven and I say, I won't be defeated!" I've kept that with me a long time.

There's a little plant over there with printing on the pot that says, "I won't be defeated." That plant was one leaf, and I clipped it off a great big thing that was dying and stuck it in the ground. This whole office got hysterical because, as you can see, we're undergound—we have no windows, no light. They all laughed at me. Look at the size of that plant now. I think you have to take everything that looks like a blow and turn it into a triumph. This is where my energy comes from: I just won't be licked.

—BEVERLY SILLS, 1984

■

The powerful will and self-confidence that this story reveals is apparent immediately upon meeting Beverly Sills. Tall and solid, she gives off the air of being utterly unshakable—not a nervous giggle or fidget to be seen. She is calm, stately, large, and even a trifle stern, in spite of a curly, feminine hairdo and heavy makeup; she is a mixture of queen and mother. But her assurance also makes her easy to be with, and she laughs readily and merrily, her expressive eyebrows arching high above her lively eyes. Indeed, her face changes dramatically with her moods, perhaps a result of her many years performing the melodramas of opera, perhaps a natural talent that added to her acting. When she smiles, her round cheeks bunch up into a happy, girlish grin, which is enhanced by the reddish-blond curls that frame her head. When she is serious—and she often is—the lines circling under those cheeks pull her face down into an expression that is achingly sad. But capability radiates from her every move. She makes you, somehow, want to lay your fate in her hands.

This capability, which she probably possessed ever since the age of three, when she was already winning talent contests and doing radio shows, has been essential to her dual career as singer and opera director. As an opera singer, she has achieved one of the most distinguished careers in the field. She was a leading soprano for both the Metropolitan and New York City Operas and has sung with famous companies throughout the world, thus becoming one of the first Americans to break through the traditional prejudice that only Europeans can sing opera. When she retired from singing in 1980—"I got out while they were still fighting to buy tickets to hear me. I believe in getting out when you're on top, and that's what I did"—she became general director of the New York City Opera.

In that position, Sills has created the first home company for American singers, who have traditionally gone to Europe for training and experience. She has also embraced new, innovative operas written by young composers and has kept the company predominantly American, unlike the Metropolitan Opera, which follows the time-honored practice of importing famous European singers as its stars. She has worked to get funding and scholarships for young singers, and many in her company are Hispanic, black, or from less-than-wealthy backgrounds.

"I am responsible for everything you see and hear from the minute you walk in here!" she says with a somewhat proud laugh. "I frequently say that I never share blame, I never share credit, and I never share desserts!" Then she adds more seriously, "To run an opera company—well, it only advances by crisis. But the buck stops here."

The work of running an opera company makes Sills's days seem "endless," as she puts it. She gets up at 6:00 A.M. to make breakfast for her husband, Peter Greenough, a retired newspaper executive, and their twenty-five-year-old daughter, Muffy. She goes to her office in Lincoln Center at 8:30 and spends an hour dictating letters and memos. Then she begins an eternal round of fundraising activities, rehearsals, production meetings, and decision making. She takes no lunch, unless it is part of a fundraising event, and if there's a performance she must watch it either in the theater or on her closed-circuit television, so the day doesn't end until 11:00 P.M. If there is no performance, she collapses into bed at 9:00.

"Sometimes, I feel just plain sleepy," she admits.

She tries to get home for dinner, so that she can at least have a couple of hours with her family, but often her husband and daughter have to meet her at Lincoln Center and take her out for the meal. Sometimes her husband brings his books and sits quietly in the office with Sills as she works.

Because she spends so much time at work, Sills has decorated her office to look like a home. It is a surprising sight, for the rest of the "backstage" area of the opera house, which is really underground, has the cold, institutional look of a hospital: corridors of white tile and brown metal lockers in dim electric light. Her living-room-like office is clearly a haven: overstuffed chairs, couches, and a chaise lounge rest on the thick carpet, knickknacks given to her by fans crowd the coffee table, and posters of past operas adorn the walls. On one wall hangs a lush blue-velvet curtain that sweeps from ceiling to floor. It is embroidered with elaborately bejeweled queens, representing the many queens Sills has played in her operatic roles. "I'm here so much and so long that sometimes, I'll stretch out on that chair and put the light on and do my work, just so that I can get the feeling that I'm not surrounded by desks and typewriters" she says.

Beverly Sills did not have the beginnings one might expect of an opera "superstar," as the press has often labeled her. Born Belle Miriam Silverman fifty-five years ago, she grew up in what was then a typical middle-class Jewish area of Brooklyn—Coney Island. It was a far-from-affluent neighborhood, and the family often experienced hard times.

"At one time we had to move to a one-bedroom apartment," Sills recalls, "and the three of us slept in the hallway. My two brothers shared a hide-a-bed and I slept on a cot. We only had a radio because my grandfather built us one, and when my father got a car, the whole neighborhood had a ride in it. And we all wore hand-me-downs. But my father made a good living and we never went without food."

Her father, a Rumanian Jew who came to this country as an infant ("I don't want to forget that I have some gypsy blood in me," Sills says, "I kind of like that"), was the undisputed head of the household. He laid down the law, was served first at every dinner party, paid all the bills, and even accompanied his wife when she went clothes shopping. "She never paid a bill in her life!" Sills says, laughing. "When she went to buy her clothes, he went with her. He thought she was the most beautiful woman he'd ever seen and he told everybody so. He loved to dress her and take her and show her off, and she really was beautiful. In the early days, when

I was auditioning—it was the time of Shirley Temple and all the child stars—we'd go to the movie companies and they were really much more interested in my mother than in me. She was really a knockout."

In spite of her father's old-fashioned values, he encouraged his only daughter to achieve in school as much as his two sons.

"He gave me my sense of discipline," she says. "He didn't have any respect for people who would not finish what they had set out to do. He was also very practical." He made her go to summer camp once, for example, because he wanted her to have interests other than singing, in case that didn't work out for her. "You can't be single-minded about anything," he told her.

When Sills won the Most Distinguished Athlete Award at camp that summer, her father was proud. When she got top grades throughout school and showed an amazing aptitude for languages —by the age of ten she could speak French, Italian, and a little Russian—he was proud, too. He wanted her to be smart. But he never dreamed of her being an opera star. He didn't approve when she began doing radio commercials and programs as a child. The dream of being an opera singer come from her mother.

"My mother wasn't a stage mother, but she gave us the dream that we could be anything we wanted, that nothing was out of our reach and that she was there to help us achieve whatever the dream was. And that's exactly how it turned out—we all became what we set out to be, and it's all due to her. My mother is without question the most dominating force in my life."

The discipline from her father, the dream from her mother— perhaps the perfect combination for the making of success. Yet, probably none of it would have come to anything if Sills herself hadn't had an extraordinary drive and an extraordinary gift—her voice. When did she realize that she had such a talent?

"I knew later, not right away. When I was three, I was having such a good time singing and tap dancing and going on the radio and my Mama making me pretty dresses—it was just a lot of fun. It was really much later, when I began to listen to my mother's collection of recordings, that I got terribly enthralled with the sound of a trained human voice.

"My mother took me to my first opera when I was eight, and I was hooked. I thought it was the most beautiful thing I'd ever heard and I only knew that I wanted to sing like that and be on that stage. And when I told my mother, she hadn't the slightest idea how to begin. She was only giving me singing and tap dancing and piano lessons because she thought all little girls should do those things. What do you do with a child of eight with such an ambition? If you discuss it with anyone, they look at the child as if she's some sort of monster. And I wasn't. I was just a nice little kid who wanted to be an opera singer!

"When I began to push to learn opera, my mother found me a teacher, Miss Liebling. It turned out to be so expensive my father just couldn't afford it—singing lessons were for daughters of very rich people. So I helped pay for it by doing radio commercials and, later, I sang in an after-hours club for tips. But Miss Liebling became terribly interested in me and let my father pay what he could. In a sense, she was my patron, which was very unusual in those days.

"But I didn't really become engrossed with my own voice till I was about twelve. I couldn't get over what I could do! Suddenly I was hearing it, and it wasn't a baby voice anymore. It was like suddenly looking down and you have bosoms! I put on my mother's Galli-Curci and Lily Pons recordings and found that I could do all the scales and fancy things they were doing! I thought, 'I can do what they can do!' I didn't realize what quality meant yet. As far as I was concerned, if they could turn three somersaults, I could, too. The fact that I finished up landing on my behind and they were landing standing up and looking like ballerinas didn't enter my mind!"

But her gift for singing was not all she had. She was also able to learn an entire operatic role in three or four days—another remarkable talent. And she could devote herself to work in a way that few children that age ever can.

"My life literally changed when I was about ten or eleven because I dropped my friends. I was so hooked on this art form that I spent all my time in the library, looking up operas, the lives of composers." Impatient with her inability to read operas in Italian, she paid a man in the neighborhood fifty cents an hour to teach her. "Reading just opened up a whole new world to me, and I was ready to move."

When she was twelve, Sills's parents put a stop to her life in "show biz" because they wanted her to have a more normal existence. She did—she was popular in school, did well in her studies, and had a boyfriend—but she still devoted every spare minute to music, singing and learning operas. She also kept auditioning for operatic and chorus parts, and she got almost everything she tried out for. But, until she was fifteen, her father wouldn't hear of her going on stage. "First you go to college, then try the stage," he insisted. Finally, however, when she got a chance to tour Europe singing in a Gilbert and Sullivan repertory, he gave in. To make it up to him, she won a mathematics scholarship to Fairleigh Dickinson College before she left.

Sills was never to take advantage of that scholarship or to go to college, for her career quickly took off. By the time she was nineteen, she was an opera singer. Looking back now, how much does she thing her success was due to her talent and how much to sheer hard work?

"Well, I think having a singing voice is a unique talent. It's kind of like a diamond. You can't manufacture a diamond—if you do, it's a fake. But, it does have to be polished and put in its proper setting in order to be appreciated. In the case of a creative talent such as singing or painting, I think quite a lot is God-given. Then it is honed and polished on earth.

"But opera is a highly disciplined art form. You have to know at least two languages, you have to be a musician. It's a lifetime of study and discipline, not just an overnight thing."

Many people don't realize this. Movies and gossip magazines habitually depict opera stars as leading glamorous and fast lives.

"Forget all that—it's all a joke!" Sills exclaims. "You can't sing with a hangover, you can't sing with a sore throat from a lot of smoking. You can't sing if you're tired because breath control is the key to all singing, and you get winded. It's a very athletic art form, and you have to be fit. It's not an art form that goes on in spite of the way you feel either, it goes on *because* of the way you feel. Yelling at football games is not for a singer. Nor is yelling at the children! My children were blessed because I was so aware of those vocal chords that I never raised my voice!"

Sills laughs her merry laugh, and leans back against the couch. Cool and unruffled in a plain white summer dress, she nevertheless looks weary. Her lifetime of discipline is apparent in her controlled demeanor, and her fifty-odd years of singing can be heard in the huskiness of her voice.

With a life that has always been and still is so busy, it is hard for Sills to find the time to relax. She tries to take six weeks off a year now, although the opera's schedule never allows her to take the time all at once, and during the season she never gets a Sunday off because there are always two performances that day. Her favorite forms of relaxation are doing jigsaw puzzles, playing word games with her husband, and playing bridge with friends. But getting adequate time to spend with her family has never been easy, and she has a lot of family—three stepdaughters, her own two children, and now grandchildren as well.

"The question is always put to me, 'How did you manage to have it all—career and family?'" she says, a little sadly. "Well, I didn't have it all. When you go for all, somebody pays the price. In my case, I think my daughter Muffy paid the price because I was away so much. I kept her with me a lot—by the time she was five, she'd been around the world three times—but I think growing up well was a challenge for her.

"Still, there was one mistake I didn't make. I always let my husband and children know that if at any time they wanted me to stop what I was doing, I would stop. They never asked me to, so I guess I was lucky."

Sometimes, though, there were difficult clashes between family and career demands. With a mixture of amusement and regret, Sills describes two such occasions.

"Once, when I was ready to go out to sing a performance of *The Magic Flute*, I went to say goodbye to one of my daughters, who was miserable with a fever and a cold. I was all dressed up because there was going to be a little opening-night party in the theater afterward. I leaned down, she put her arms around me, I picked her up out of bed, and she threw up all over me!" Sills grimaces.

"So I cleaned us both up, put on a pair of old pants and a shirt, and went down to the theater and sang. I never went to the party." Sills pauses, thinks for a moment, then shrugs. "There are moments when you just can't imagine how you get your act together to go on. I was once so tired from having stayed up all night with the children—three of them had measles and it was like a little hospital ward at home—that, after I did my first aria, I walked off the stage into the dressing room door and gave myself a black eye. I was too tired to realize the door was half open. In between that aria and the next there is about a thirty-minute lapse—this was also *The Magic Flute*—and people ran with ice cubes and everything. The second aria is very hard, and I did it very badly. Sometimes, it is just impossible."

Sills's problems as a mother were not only ordinary ones, however. One of her stepdaughters and both her own children have disabilities. Muffy is deaf; one stepdaughter is mentally retarded; and her son, Bucky, is deaf, autistic, epileptic, and mentally retarded. She found out about her son's handicaps when he was a baby, only two months after receiving the stunning news that her daughter was deaf. Yet, even in the face of these tragedies—and perhaps partly because of them—she has held on to her refusal to be defeated.

"I've always found that at the very pit, and I've been to the pit a lot, there's something that pulls you back up," she says intensely, the sad lines showing again. "I don't know if we're all assigned a little guardian angel or what, but I believe you can only be defeated by yourself, and I don't believe in self-defeat. They told me Bucky would never feed himself—he feeds himself. They told me he would never be toilet trained—he's toilet trained. And he's twenty-three years old, so don't think *that* wouldn't have been catastrophic. They said that the drugs to control his epilepsy were in their infancy and wouldn't work well. This was twenty-one years ago, and today they're not in their infancy and he is controlled. His autism—we're reaching him. He's been taught six signs that they use for the deaf, so he's finally communicating.

"And if I've given my daughter nothing else, I've given her [the belief] that she isn't going to be licked either. She's a crackerjack athlete because when she started saying, 'I can't do this 'cause I can't hear the commands, I can't do that 'cause I can't hear what my teammates are doing'—I said, 'Your prowess, your capabilities have nothing to do with other people.' So she has to be twice as alert as the next guy, so what? They said it would take her years to learn to speak—she speaks. She said, how could she be an artist? Now she's designing comic books. She designs *Superman* and *Batman* and other comics, and she's very good at it. She wanted to travel but was worried about traveling alone. I said fine, join a group. I don't accept from her, 'I can't, I can't.' I don't believe in handicaps!"

Because of the problems her children have, Sills became the National Chairwoman of the Mothers' March on Birth Defects for the March of Dimes in 1972. She helped to raise $70 million within ten years and, unlike many celebrities, she hasn't just lent her name, she's really worked. She visits hospitals, meets the parents of birth-defected children, fundraises, and spends time with the children themselves. In her autobiography, *Bubbles*, there is a photograph of her that acutely expresses her sadness. She is half turned toward the camera, reaching down toward a child in a wheelchair, her eyes fixed on him. Her brow is furrowed and the lines that encircle her cheeks are deeper than ever. In that picture, she is not a star—there is no thought for herself or her looks. She quite plainly just hurts.

Yet, she has enjoyed the work, and says that if she had chosen a career other than singing, it probably would have been in the social services, an avocation that is evident in the work she does do. She has, for example, initiated a program to bring opera to disadvantaged children in their own environments. She sends out busloads of singers with costumes and props to schools, where they perform a forty-five-minute excerpt from an opera. According to Sills, they are reaching about 35,000 children a year now in New York State.

"I don't believe in busing children into Lincoln Center and showing them this glamorous, gorgeous theater that they might never go into again. I believe in bringing it to them in their ambiance so that it becomes part of their everyday life. I'd like them to know that every week, somebody's going to come and tell them a story and sing to them a little bit. I don't care if they become opera lovers or rock lovers, it's just that music should be an integral part of their lives."

She has also worked to make the New York City Opera available to people who like it, regardless of how poor they are.

"People think, 'Opera—big, fat ladies with horns coming out of their heads. That's dead and buried," she says vehemently. "Opera is not just for the rich lady who has lots of pearls around her neck."

Opera was originally a popular, family entertainment, and in most of Italy it still is. Opera companies tour the country and perform in large theaters for low prices. People come with food and wine and, instead of acting hushed and reverent like American audiences, they cheer the heroes, boo the villains, and throw flowers at the heroines. Grown men cry at the tragedies, and everyone jumps up and down and yells at the end. Sills wants to revive this spirit in the New York City Opera, so she sells tickets for $5.50 and up, instead of the $75 they can cost at the Metropolitan; sometimes special performances sell for even less. She has seats in the Standing Room Only sections, so that no one has to be uncomfortable, and she is constantly seeking out corporations willing to underwrite tickets to make them even cheaper. In a truly revolutionary move, she has hung a screen above the stage on which the words of the opera are translated into English, so that everyone can follow the story. Her view is that people should be able to enjoy opera, regardless of how they are dressed or how much they know about music.

"My only requirement for people who come into the theater is that they come with the idea that they would like to have a good time!"

The innovations Sills has introduced have brought criticism as well as praise. Indeed, throughout her life she has been more subject than most to the opinions of others, because she has so long been in the public eye. How does she cope with criticism?

"Well, it all starts with self-belief. You simply have to believe that you are good at what you do and that what you do is special. I think each one of us is special; otherwise God would have made us all alike. Isn't it interesting that there are no two voices that are exactly alike?

"When I sang a good performance, it didn't matter what was said about it. You could not take that performance away from me. On the other hand, if I gave a bad performance, and I read the next day that it was good, it was still bad. You couldn't take that away from me either, or the ache in my heart from knowing that I had done a second-rate job. But I just don't accept other people putting the stamp of defeat on me. They don't have a right to do that. Only I do. And I just don't punish myself by agreeing with people who don't like me!"

She sits back, the determined, triumphant note in her voice still echoing in the room. She seems to be catching her breath, for she has been speaking fast and passionately.

"I don't think my opinion is worth less than anybody else's," she continues. "I don't know anybody who's in that superior a position to me. There's nobody on earth! I came on earth with as much as they've got." She smiles again, then says almost ferociously, "In whatever I do, I do as best I can, and I don't owe anybody any more!"

SILLS COMMENTARY

B everly Sills was an easy person to profile because she talks like a book. Candid, clear, amusing, she is a natural storyteller— my twenty-two pages of transcribed interview read almost as well as a written autobiography. She has no difficult accent to decipher, no habit of winding away on distracting diatribes—she is always quotable. The one problem was her fame. She was so used to being interviewed: how was I going to get something different?

I collected the usual wad of files on her from the library, plowed through the interviews, and read her autobiography, *Bubbles* (her nickname). Naturally, I was struck by the tragedies she had undergone in her personal life—a singer, a lover of music, whose children were both deaf; a highly accomplished, brilliant woman whose son was retarded and autistic..The juxtaposition of the effervescent image of "Bubbles" with these private tragedies intrigued me, and I wanted to explore them. But I was also struck by the fact that she'd been in the public eye since she was three. What is it, I began to wonder, that makes people like Sills ambitious and successful? Where did her drive and talent originate? Was she pushed by someone, or did she push herself? Where did she get the confidence to keep trying, even in the face of defeat? Is there something different in the life of highly successful people that makes them able to push so far above the crowd? These questions were not the ones Sills had usually been asked. Perhaps, I thought, this theme could make the piece different.

Sills made the interview easy for me because she was unabashed and not at all secretive about her struggles. She spoke honestly and with affection about her childhood, her parents, and her career. The only time I felt she dissembled was when I asked her whether she was attracted to the idea of being famous as a child, and she insisted that she didn't see opera singers as associated with fame. "I had no idea these were famous people, I just knew that whatever that woman was doing, I wanted to do."

As I listened to Sills, I quickly began to see the power of her will. It was hard to know whether that power was a result of being used to fame or was an attribute that pushed her toward the fame to begin with, but it was unmistakable. She had the same kind of hard-edged confidence I would see in Susan Sontag but was much more at ease with her prominence. She was clearly used to being a boss, to being obeyed, and to being efficient. She was not the sort of person one would easily cross.

As the interview went on, I began to notice other sides of her personality that might have made her "different," too. Her irrepressible humor, her articulateness, her intelligence, her talent, her "presence," and her extraordinary level of energy. She was, in many ways, larger than life.

I also discovered another aspect of her fame as we talked—a set of pet peeves she was going to bring up regardless of my questions. (People who are used to being interviewed often have a range of pat statements they depend upon to get them through interviews. I don't think Sills was particularly guilty of this, but I was wary of the danger. As said earlier, the only way around this is to study up on one's subject enough to find the questions that will elicit original answers.) One of her pet peeves was the importance of family life. "Don't forget I was born fifty-five years ago and 'women's lib' was an absolutely unknown phrase," she said. "So, although I'm very enthusiastic about the liberation movement, the liberation of the woman's mind is what I'm enthusiastic about. I'm not enthusiastic about the destruction of the family unit." She talked about the importance of family, in her own life and in general, for pages.

"There are so many changes from the time that I grew up," she said. "We were more physically affectionate, very demonstrative. There was nothing self-conscious about it. Now we have such difficulty with relationships that, if we see two men earnestly talking with one another, we immediately decide that they are homosexual. Two women walking down the street holding hands, we immediately think they are gay women. But when we were kids it was a very affectionate society. I never saw my brothers leave the house without kissing my father goodbye, even when they were adults."

Sills also was unstoppable when she got into memories of her childhood. Her father died when she was twenty, leaving her obviously sad that he didn't live to see how his children and grandchildren have done, and in a sense she seemed to be reiterating her memories for him. She glowed with love for her parents.

"They were a marvellous team," she recalled. "He had a volatile temper, she had no temper at all—always cheerful, always giggling and laughing. She's sixty now, and she still giggles! She could talk him in and out of anything. But he could shoot off in a second. It wasn't frightening, though.

"I remember we all had chores. My oldest brother's chore was to take the garbage out. There were no disposables, none of the big, fancy garbage bags—it was really a kind of unpleasant task. My mother had asked my older brother several times to do it and he just didn't, so finally she lifted up this heavy thing and took it out herself.

"My father waited until the next night at dinner. We were all seated and suddenly he got up and went over to the garbage pail, took out the bag of garbage and put it in the middle of the dining room table, right in front of my brother. My brother looked up and my father said to him, 'Since you seem to enjoy living with it so much, you might as well eat it.' So my brother took the garbage out after that!"

The only drawback to Sills's volubility was that it made it difficult for me to maintain control of the interview. I would ask her a question such as "How did your mother influence your ambitions?" and she would go off into a fifteen-minute digression on the importance of fathers as role models. I would then have to steer her back by fishing out a point she'd just made and applying it to my next question. "But it seems that the combination of your parents' personalities was ideal for encouraging ambition." Or, "Talking about discipline, I wanted to ask you how much you think talent is innate, and how much of it is plain work?"

As for tackling the delicate question of her children, she made that easy for me, too. I had planned to wait until we had been talking for some time—until we were both comfortable—to bring it up, but she jumped the gun on me and mentioned it first. Once she had opened the subject, it enabled me to draw her out on her philosophy of life and how she has managed to keep going in the face of tragedy. As she spoke about her children, I saw the same relentless determination to do her best for them that she had used to realize her ambitions. When she went into her speech about God and fate and optimism, ending with the story about Rose Kennedy and the plant that wouldn't be defeated with which I opened the piece, I realized that my two themes—the tragic history behind the happy mask, and how a person gets famous—had finally united. Beverly Sills, I saw, was hard and serious and fierce under the charm. She was, as my title reflected, undefeatable.

I had been assigned this profile by the New York City Commission on the Status of Women, which was putting together a book called *Women Making History,* a collection of fifteen portraits of New York women designed for use in high schools throughout New York State. I and four co-authors were told not to write down to the teenage audience but to make sure to emphasize aspects of our subjects that might be inspirational to our young readers. The book was supposed to provide role models to high school girls, and thus it encompassed profiles of women in all different fields, from all sorts of ethnic, racial, and economic backgrounds. (Some of the other profiles, for instance, were of a Puerto Rican doctor, Maria

Rodriguez-Trias; newscaster Charlayne Hunter-Gault; vice-presidential candidate Geraldine Ferraro; and handicapped marathon champion Linda Down.) This brings up another point I haven't yet mentioned—the demands of the market. As "free" as profile writers are to interpret their subjects, the market—the house style of the magazine, the editor's perceptions of the readers' tastes and prejudices—still controls the form, and to some extent, the language of the piece. Had I been writing a profile of Beverly Sills for *New York Woman*, it probably would have been more irreverent and gossipy; for the *New Yorker*, more thorough, with more emphasis on backstage at the opera; for a music magazine, more technical.

Looking back on this and on the other four profiles I did for that book, I regret that I was forced to write them so fast. If one is to regard a profile as a complete portrait, as a record for posterity— and now that Sills is retired from her position of director of the New York City Opera this piece does take on the aspect of history —one wants it to be thorough. My twenty-two pages of notes contain a lot more of her than I managed to get across in this relatively small, tight piece.

FOUR

Filling Silences with Strong Voices

.

PAULE MARSHALL

As a child, the writer Paule* Marshall sat in the kitchen of her Brooklyn brownstone, listening to her West Indian mother talk with friends for hours. She listened half against her will, absorbing not only the women's language, which was lilting, colorful, and poetic, but their message. "You got to take yuh mouth and make a gun," as the women used to say.

"The women I grew up with were larger-than-life figures to me," Marshall says now. "But as I grew older and had my own encounters with the ways society let me know that it saw me as 'a lesser person,' I began to realize that the talk in the kitchen was a way for those women to reassert themselves, to deny the image that the world had of them. I began to understand the attitude of society toward all of us black women—sexism and racism. And I also began to realize that I didn't see myself or those strong women reflected anywhere in literature."

Ever since, Marshall's mission as a writer has been, as she explains it, to present these strong, black women to the world.

Selina, for example, the young heroine of Marshall's first novel, *Brown Girl, Brownstones* (1959), struggles against the stifling future her mother and community plan for her and wins independence. Merle, the dynamic protagonist of the second novel, *The Chosen Place, the Timeless People* (1969), takes the troubles of her people to heart, yet bears up with defiance and wit. And Avey Johnson, the

* Paule is pronounced Paul.

uptight heroine of Marshall's latest novel, *Praisesong for the Widow* (1983), moves from naïve acceptance of all things American to an enlightened questioning. These are just the heroines; many more strong women populate Marshall's novels and stories.

"When I started writing *Brown Girl, Brownstones*," Marshall says, "I had the sense that the world of those women was just passing away, and I wanted to get it down on paper before it all vanished. . . . Black women are so remarkable! It's important that their story be told."

Marshall herself easily qualifies as the kind of woman whom people refer to as "strong." She isn't imposing—not particularly tall, slightly built, youthful for her fifty-five years, and pretty, with high cheekbones, wide eyes, and only a touch of gray in her short, natural hairstyle. But despite a light, gentle voice, she gives the impression of being someone you don't fool with. She concentrates intensely as she talks, speaking in spurts and taking long pauses as she selects her words, and she seems supremely self-reliant. Her life now is somewhat solitary, with her son grown and living in Newport, Rhode Island, designing boats, and her husband long since divorced from her, but she appears to have chosen it that way. She says she disliked talking on the telephone and sees friends only occasionally. When she is at home and not off teaching at one university or another, her life is her work.

"When I'm really involved in writing a book, I try to get started on it early and work from about 8:00 o'clock to 1:30 or so," she says in her soft voice. "Then I take a leisurely lunch, maybe a nap and a read, and a walk. By then the day is pretty much over. When I've put in that morning of work, I need the rest of the day to recover!" She laughs suddenly, a flash of lightness breaking through her reserve. Then she adds, serious again, "It's a very simple and rather dull life, apart from the work."

Marshall's work, as she calls her writing, has not come easily. Having to support herself and bring up her son alone has eaten into her writing time—one of the reasons, she says, she has produced relatively little. And she writes slowly. "I have to work all day to produce half a page that I won't throw out the next day." Also, for most of her writing years, her work was critically successful but not commercially so. Even though today's long-overdue interest in women's writing is now bringing her belated attention, her lack of funds still shows in the way she lives. From her apartment on the unfashionable upper reaches of Central Part West, where she has lived for twenty-five years, you can hear the A train rumbling below at regular intervals. She owns no car and, as she says, "no fur coats."

"As a writer you learn to live on the edge financially," she says. Marshall supports herself by teaching at various universities and colleges around the country for six months out of every year, an existence she calls "uncomfortable."

The apartment itself, although not fancy and in a run-down neighborhood, is pleasant. Her living room, facing Central Park, is painted a dark, creamy yellow, enhanced by the deep brown of her wooden furniture, the leather couch, and the glossy black grand piano in one corner. A tall, lush plant stands near the piano, a pretty blue bottle of Jamaican rum rests in a basket next to the couch, and the walls are decorated with posters announcing African art shows and a painting of black field workers. The apartment rather neatly combines an atmosphere of city life with the tropical lushness of the West Indies. The place represents, for Marshall, the embodiment of a childhood dream.

"I'm a real Brooklyn girl," she says, smiling. "I was born right on Fulton Street—my mother didn't get to hospital fast enough. I went to junior high and high school in Brooklyn, and eventually to Brooklyn College. During the time I grew up there, in the section that's now known as Bed-Stuy, Brooklyn was known as the borough of churches and baby carriages, and to my mind, it was the dullest place in the world. My great ambition was to cross the East River and move to Manhattan."

Yet, Marshall's childhood world was not all that typical, nor all that dull. She may have been "just a Brooklyn girl" while out on the streets, speaking Brooklyn Black English with her friends, but once she stepped into her brownstone house, all that changed.

"Then I instantly became a West Indian, even with the accent!" she says. "The power of the world that those women created in that house, the West Indian world, was so strong that I had this dual cultural experience from the very beginning. My books come out of different needs, but they're all part of an ongoing effort to reconcile those dual cultures, and to define what it is to be a black woman in the world."

Marshall temporarily escaped from Brooklyn when she was grown, got rid of both Brooklyn and Barbados accents to avoid being teased (something she now regrets), and enrolled at Hunter College in Manhattan. Yet, she found herself still in a trap, for in those days, the late 1940s, women were expected to major either in English, with the goal of teaching elementary school, or in social work. Marshall fell in with the expected and became a pre–social work major, ignoring her hidden desire to write.

In her sophomore year, however, her life changed. She became seriously ill and had to leave college for a year. She went upstate to rest, read, and ruminate.

"I realized that I liked people but I didn't want to work with them. I didn't want to be a social worker!" she says, clasping her knee and leaning back against the couch. "I remember writing to a friend at that time, describing the part of the country where I was living, and he wrote back and said it was such a beautifully de-scribed scene, why didn't I think of writing? It was as if he had signaled the thing in me that I had been unable to admit, even unconsciously."

So, tentatively, she decided to drop social work and switch to an English major with an emphasis in creative writing. She gave up Hunter and Manhattan and transferred to Brooklyn College.

After she was graduated, Marshall decided to buck tradition and look for a job in journalism or publishing, which her guidance counselor told her was plain foolhardiness. This was in 1953, a time when there were almost no blacks in top jobs. She looked for almost two years, getting to know "Publisher's Row" on Madison Avenue so well that, she says, "You could have put me on the corner of Forty-second Street and Madison blindfolded, and I could have found any of those places." She tried *Mademoiselle, Time, Life,* various publishing houses, and everything in between over and over again, getting nowhere. She calls it an agonizing experience, and has recreated it in *Praisesong for the Widow,* where Jay, Avey's husband, tries hopelessly to find a job as an accountant.

"The thing that used to outrage me the most was the fact that they never really intended to give me the job," she says now, her jaw setting slightly. "There was a ritual that took place in nearly all the offices: they'd send out for tea or coffee and sit with me and chat. They would make some positive sounds about my record in school, the fact that I graduated Phi Beta Kappa from college, and sometimes, I'd be on my way down in the elevator before it had actually gotten through to me that I had not been offered the job!"

Nevertheless, with a determination and drive born, perhaps, out of her Barbadian background, Marshall persisted. Finally, one day, walking along Forty-third Street, she happened to glance up and see a sign in a dingy window that said OUR WORLD MAGAZINE. She knew it to be a kind of "second-rate *Ebony*" that she had seen in dentists' offices. On the spur of the moment, she walked in and asked to see the editor.

"And strangely enough, he was willing. I think he was a little amazed by my audacity for those days," Marshall laughs. "He was a brilliant man, a black man by the name of John Davis, a Rhodes scholar. He was kind of taken with me and said, 'Well, what do you think you know?' I said, 'I know absolutely nothing. I'm just trying to get some experience by getting a job!' So he said, 'Okay, I'll give you a chance.' "

She was hired, first as a researcher, and before long, as a writer. In some ways, the job was glamorous—she was sent to the West Indies and Brazil to cover stories, put in charge of Foods and Fashion—and it taught her to write quickly and under pressure, but, deep down, she was dissatisfied. The emphasis of the magazine on the high life of entertainers, on trivia, frustrated her. She longed to write about something more serious.

"So, in sheer desperation, I went home one evening and started working on *Brown Girl, Brownstones* in the hope of providing an antidote to what I was doing all day long. In a sense, it was a novel waiting to be written. That first draft was a real kind of out-pouring."

Unlike many writers, Marshall did not entertain dreams of fame and glory. She didn't even dare think of publication, for, as she puts it, "Once you put it out there, you discover whether you have talent or not!" So she approached the idea of publishing gradually. She joined writers' workshops at the Harlem Writers' Guild. "I just needed to be with other people who were doing this absolutely frightening thing." And after a couple of years, when she had a 600-page manuscript lying on her desk, she finally decided to send it out.

At this stage, most writers try to find an agent who has contacts in the publishing world, but Marshall didn't know about any of that. She simply picked up the telephone book, looked up "Publishing Houses" in the yellow pages, and took the first name off the list she recognized—Bobbs-Merrill. She bundled up her tome and sent it off. It languished on the editor's desk, unread, for a year, keeping Marshall on agonizing tenterhooks.

"I was in a dilemma. On the one hand, maybe their keeping it so long meant they were interested. On the other hand, I wanted to pick up the phone and say, if you don't want it, send it back."

At last she heard from the editor. He said he was interested but was having trouble with the company. A while later, her manuscript came back, rejected. The editor had left.

"But I still hadn't learned my lesson!" Marshall says with a proud tilt of her head. She sent it off to Random House. And they wanted it.

"My editor said that when I received my advance, which was something like $2,500, I was to take my bloated manuscript and go off somewhere and extricate the lovely novel that was buried in the fat," she says.

But this was the early 1950s, a time that was not receptive to black writers, especially female ones, as Marshall soon found out.

"The day I received my contract in the mail, I was so excited! It was the same day that I had a meeting with my editor to talk about the changes that were needed in the manuscript. I was so elated! Contract in hand, I went over to meet him. On the way, I ran into a Random House executive. He stopped to have a few words with me, and the upshot of his remarks was that he said in parting, after the usual pleasantries, 'Oh, you know, nothing very much happens with this kind of book.'

"I was utterly devastated. The contract I had in my hand felt like a rejection slip." Marshall stops talking, frowns, and stares ahead at the wall.

"As I've reflected on it over the years, it seemed to me that he was not only saying that Random House wasn't going to put much into publicizing and pushing that book, but he was saying something which has to do with women and writers, especially black women: that, as far as he was concerned, the book wasn't really part of American letters." She pauses and shut her eyes for a moment, as if to defuse her feelings. "He was so mistaken. *Brown Girl, Brownstones* is a kind of classic American novel. It's a novel of immigrants, problems of adjustment and acculturation and so on; it was just that in this case the immigrants happened to black. It was also typically American in that it's the story of a young woman coming of age—a rite of passage. It is *supremely* a part of American letters!"

Marshall's anger and defiance about injustice figure largely in her books. But her major aim as a writer is not so much to "take yuh mouth and make a gun" as to capture the lives of the people she knows and show them in all their humanity.

"There is a kind of thinking current in this society that blacks spend twenty-four hours a day reacting to the institutionalized racism of America, that we're totally defined by racism," she says carefully, now fanning herself with a palm fan, now picking at the white fur draped over the back of her couch. "I didn't want to give that impression in *Brown Girl, Brownstones*. I wanted to deal first of all with Selina simply growing up and struggling with her parents, with her background, with her sexuality—I wanted these things to figure in her life before that whole question of racism.

"So, first of all, I want my work to reveal the black people and the black community to themselves, to itself, so that young black people going to the library will not have the experience I did, which was that there were no books about *me*. I want them to see themselves reflected through the fiction and stories because there's something marvelous and magical when that happens. It gives them a sense of their right to *be* in this world." Marshall pauses again, thinking, still and serious.

"The other thing is that, although like most writers, I write what I know, I am also involved with universal themes, so I hope that the work will give those who are nonblack a sense of other worlds, other peoples, and what the similarities and differences are—so that, through the understanding of the humanity of that world, they will be influenced to be better people. . . .

"One of the gratifying things about my work is that, so far, it has done that," she continues, relaxing now into a smile. "Black people go to my work and they say, 'You know, that's for real. The same thing happened to me. I *know* that person!' There's nothing more gratifying for a writer! And, at the same time, I get people who are not of my background empathizing with the story because it strikes this universal chord. With Selina, for example—yes, she is a young black woman growing up in Brooklyn, but her struggles with her mother and her determination to be her own person are universal."

Marshall recrosses her legs and adjusts her simple red sundress. Then, with a slight nod and a grunt of triumph she concludes, "And achieving that universal reaction has been what the goal of my work is all about."

MARSHALL COMMENTARY

Paule Marshall granted me a gracious but impersonal interview, one of the most impersonal I have had. She was clearly an extremely private person, not eager for publicity, not eager to give her writing time over to an interviewer, not eager to reveal anything about her personal life to a stranger. If I had not been interviewing her for a good cause—the New York City Commission on the Status of Women's book for high school students—I doubt she would have granted me the interview at all.

By impersonal, I mean that she hardly engaged directly with me at all. She spoke to the wall, rarely glancing at my face, and she became deeply absorbed in her own careful answers and thoughts. Sometimes she even closed her eyes as she spoke.

I wrote in my notes afterward: "She sits still, hardly moving except to fan herself with a palm leaf, to adjust the skirt of her red, delicately striped sundress, or to turn to look at me. She talks very slowly, thinking out each word as she goes, sometimes taking long pauses that make you think she's lost track, although she hasn't.

"As she talks, she changes. Sometimes she is gentle, kind. Sometimes grim, sometimes laughingly sassy. She seems like someone who is solitary and yet likes it. Someone who has a rich inner life, private and reserved, yet is neither bitter nor sad. She seems fulfilled yet maybe a touch lonely."

Because of her remove from me, I decided not to use the first person singular in my piece. My presence seemed irrelevant, in a way. I could have been anyone, even just a tape recorder asking her questions. She was so self-contained, so absorbed, so serious, that I didn't feel that I, as the reporter, belonged in the story.

The question of whether to use "I" in a story is an important one in profile writing and one I have not yet dealt with. Although, traditionally, the "I" is supposed to be avoided in journalism— especially in newspaper journalism—it is often impossible to do so. No one denies that the profile writer affects his or her subject. In the Brodsky piece, for example, I felt compelled to put myself in because I believed that Brodsky had reacted to me differently than he would have to someone else, especially a man. And I could not have described him taking my coffee or scoffing at me without using the "I": "He leaned over and helped himself to this reporter's coffee" would have sounded absurd.

Likewise, I needed the "I" for Sontag, Mitford, and Singer. These people said things to me, or did things concerning me, that I could not include without using first person. Sontag took to me, it seemed, and warmed up as a result. Mitford and her husband included me in their evening routine of cocktails and chat. Singer allowed me into his secret hideout. And the more I wished to include personal observation and a chatty tone, the more I needed to rely on the "I." The "I" also frees the writer—and New Journalists recognized this —to use a casual, daring, independent style.

In the Beverly Sills piece, however, I felt, as I did with Marshall, that the "I" was not necessary. Her quotations were a result of my questions, yes, but there was no special event or unique interplay that required me to be in the story. Instead I used direct questions in that piece—such as "When did she realize that she had such a talent?"—but put them in third person, without the "I asked." Likewise, with Marshall, my presence to her was no more than the presence of a reporter, so "I" did not belong.

During the interview with Marshall, I became particularly intrigued by two of her statements: that she wrote in order to make characters that were recognizable to everyone, universal; and that blacks are not defined by racism, and do not spend twenty-four hours a day thinking and talking about it. I saw that she wished to present her characters first as people with universal problems and only secondarily as blacks struggling in a racist world: that, to put it simply, she wanted to combat the racist habits of our society by presenting her characters as people rather than types. But I also saw that she had a more literary ambition: to create a literature of black women where one had not really existed before, and indeed, *Brown Girl, Brownstone* came out long before Alice Walker's *The Color Purple*, or Toni Morrison's *Tar Baby* and *Beloved*. So, although she wanted to write universal books, she also wanted to write books that had special appeal to black readers. I did not think these two aims of hers clashed, however. The characters in her novels are sympathetic individuals way before they are members of categories. I therefore decided that the strong black women of her novels were a natural symbol with which to open my piece, for they encompassed both Marshall's aim to write about black women and her aim to write characters that everyone could identify with.

Marshall also made it clear to me that she had no wish to be depicted as a Struggling Black herself. She didn't want to be subject to the usual white demand that she talk about racism. She didn't want to be sacrificed to the assumption that racism is the only true subject that can exist between blacks and whites. Indeed, when I asked her about such things, she seemed impatient, almost bored. This brings me to a delicate point. There are a lot of special difficulties to be surmounted in cross-racial interviews. The interviewer can err in many ways. The most obvious, of course, is to force the subject into an unflattering stereotype, but the other side of that is to bend too far the other way and define a "minority" as perpetual victim, a perpetual sufferer of discrimination and torment, or a "majority" as a perpetual dominator of human beings —in other words, to deny the subject individuality in favor of pushing him or her into a cliché. To put it simply, blacks don't always want to be interviewed about Being Black, anymore than a white would want to be forced to talk about Being White, or a woman would want to be forced to describe Being Female. Human beings don't like to be made into symbols, and yet a profile writer is often trying to do just that. After all, no profile writer can truly capture every nuance, every detail of a person's long and complicated life. One of the biggest challenges in profile writing, therefore, is to make a point out of someone's life without oversimplifying or dehumanizing that person. As Leon Edel put it, "a writer of lives must extract individuals from their chaos, yet create an illusion that they are in the midst of life—in the way that a painter arrives at an approximation of a familiar visage on canvas. The biographer who is unable to do this creates a waxworks, a dummy, a papier-maché, and often a caricature."[1]

FIVE

Morals and Surprises

∎

PHOTOGRAPH © 1982, JERRY BAUER.

BERNARD MALAMUD

T he purpose of a writer is to keep civilization from destroying itself," Bernard Malamud once wrote,[1] and in his new novel, *God's Grace*, his intention is exactly that. The book, a fable published in 1982 by Farrar, Straus, and Giroux, is a dire warning against the perils of nuclear war and against that force within us that drives us, literally, to destroy ourselves.

"I have been concerned with this almost since the first atom bomb was dropped on the Japanese," Malamud said in a telephone interview from his house in Vermont, where he is recuperating from a serious illness. "I remember the horrid feeling I had then that the beginning of an evil time had occurred. I have a sense now, as many people have, of peril—it's terribly frightening. I feel it is the writer's business to cry havoc, because silence can't increase understanding or evoke mercy."

Malamud has written about the human struggle against destructive forces before. In his second novel, *The Assistant*, shopkeeper Morris Bober struggles against crushing poverty; in his most famous work, *The Fixer*, Yakov Bok struggles against the forces of anti-Semitism that try to destroy his freedom and his will; and in *The Tenants*, white writer Harry Lesser struggles against habits of racism when he tries to be friends with black writer Willie Spearmint. But in *God's Grace*, Malamud's eleventh book, the destructive force is the most absolute of all—nuclear war—and Malamud's conclusion the bleakest of all—utter devastation.

God's Grace opens the day after nuclear war has destroyed civilization and all human life, and the earth is smothered in one enormous flood. God, however, overlooked one man, Calvin Cohn, a paleologist who was poking around at the bottom of the sea in an oceanography vessel when the bombs blew. Cohn survives to struggle against a world destroyed by war and against that invisible force of evil in the soul that has led man to destroy himself. As God explains to him, "I made man free, but his freedom, badly used, destroyed him."

"The question of man's freedom has always interested me," Malamud said. "How much of the freedom does he have? How far does it extend? And ultimately, what does he do with it? It's the last part that bothers me most. I'm not going to gainsay man's accomplishments, but I still feel that there's a vast sense of failure that has clouded his best efforts to produce a greater freedom than he was born with."

Cohn floats on the ocean for a while, bemoaning his fate, when he discovers a companion. A baby chimpanzee named Buz has survived with him. They find an island, and soon several more apes appear, who all, through some unexplained miracle, learn how to talk. (Why can they talk? How have they survived? Is this some mysterious game of God's?) Cohn then tries to do just what Malamud suggests writers do, what he is trying to do himself with this book—stop civilization from destroying itself. He sets up a school under a tree and every day he teaches the chimps all he knows about history, science, morals, philosophy, and religion. He especially focuses on the wickedness of humankind.

"The reason I may seem to dwell a bit heavily on the negative aspect of man," he explains uncomfortably, "is to give you something to think about so you may, in a future chimpanzee society, avoid repeating man's worst errors. The future lies in your hands."

Cohn, however, is tempting God's wrath by playing with fate like this, by trying to create a new race, by, in a sense, playing God. Also, he can't resist blaming God once in a while for humankind's destruction. If God made humans imperfect, he thinks, and that imperfection led them to self-destruction, then whose fault is it? "Why didn't the Almighty do a better job?" He even argues about it with God once in a while:

"'Why do you contend with Me, Mr. Cohn?'" God booms from the sky.

". . . I humbly ask to understand the Lord's intention."

"'"Who are you to understand the Lord's intention? How can I explain my mystery to your mind? Can a cripple ascend a flaming of stars?"'"

"Abraham and Job contended," Cohn heard himself say.

"'"They were my servants."'"

"Job complained You destroyed the blameless as well as the wicked."

"'"Job therefore repented."'"

Cohn shook his enraged fist. "You have destroyed mankind. Our children are dead. Where are justice and mercy?"

Holy Moses, he thought. Am I deranged? What am I doing to me?[2]

Cohn's audacity causes him to live in fear of being struck down at any moment, and the reader lives it with him throughout the novel. By the end, Cohn has indeed gone too far. The destructive forces within him and without have caught up. The chimps revert to savagery, Cohn and his teachings are destroyed, humankind is finally extinct.

"The book asks, in a sense, a simple question," Malamud said. "Why does man treat himself so badly? What is the key to sane existence?"

This is not the first time Malamud has asked such questions. As Philip Roth once wrote of him, "What it is to be human, to be humane, is his subject; connection, indebtedness, responsibility, these are his moral concerns." He has never, however, asked them this pointedly before, nor at such a politically appropriate time—in the face of the rising possibility of nuclear war.

God's Grace is not only a serious book, it is funny. "Even a reader of holocaust drama has to be enticed into the act of reading, or he may feel he would rather forgo the anguish," Malamud said. "Not all of us are eager to be reminded of how close man has come, through his own madness, to the end of time. So, I wanted a little laughter in this serious book." He has it. The humor, some of Malamud's best, makes the novel an enticing read. Especially funny are the passages when Cohn talks back to God. At the beginning of the novel, for instance, when God finds out that Cohn has survived, they have this conversation:

"And that you, Mr. Cohn," thunders the irritated God, "happen to exist when no one else does, though embarrassing to Me, has nothing to do with your having studied for the rabbinate, or for that matter, having given it up."

Cohn ignores this reprimand and tries to bargain for his life.

"Lord . . . it wasn't as though I had a choice. I was at the bottom of the ocean attending to my work when the Devastation struck. Since I am alive it would only be fair if You let me live. A new fact is a new condition."

If Malamud were in Cohn's position, would he talk back to God like that? "Of course I would! There's a whole tradition of back-talk from Adam to Job. God may not enjoy man as much as we would like Him to, but He seems to enjoy the human voice." (With all this talk of God, one wonders if Malamud is seriously religious. All he will say is, "I think it was Carlyle who said whether he believed in God was his business and God's." A very Cohn-like answer.)

The chimps provide comedy for the novel, too, but they don't work as well as Cohn and God. Indeed, when Buz first appears, it's a little disappointing—the promise of a novel about Cohn alone in an empty world, the way Yakov Bok was alone in his prison cell in *The Fixer*, some of Malamud's best writing ever, is broken. Also, the chimps are sometimes just too cute, verging on the Walt Disneyish. This is especially true of the female chimp, who is so stereotypically feminine that she reminds one of the fluff-headed Dora in *David Copperfield*—all pout and lisp. (Her sex scenes with Cohn are bound to raise a few horrified eyebrows among readers, incidentally. They may even get the book banned, along with *The Fixer*, where the Moral Majority holds sway.) However, the interaction between the apes and Cohn becomes lively enough to make up for their occasional corniness. As Malamud said, "Talking animals can, in a sense, be exciting people."

The chimps, it turns out, not only represent the newly born race of savages in the novel, perhaps much as we must have originally been, but Christians, and so Malamud, true to form, brings in religious questions. The only ape who chooses to share Cohn's Judaism is a lumbering gorilla of questionable intelligence named George, who, like his predecessors, is rejected by the Christians. The symbolism of this—Christians as savages, the Jew as a lonely, kind-hearted outcast—might well offend some people, but Malamud does not believe in explaining his work, even to smooth ruffled tempers. To explain, he says, "destroys the art." "Why Buz is interested in Christianity and George in Judaism is their particular business," he said firmly. "But I like what has come out of it—the imaginative quality of their relationship to each other."

Malamud had the idea for the apes around 1975, while he was working on his last novel, *Dubin's Lives*. "I had done a couple of short stories about animals," he said. "One was called 'The Jewbird' and the other was 'Talking Horse,'" and I wanted to see how far I could go with that in a novel.' This experimentation is typical of Malamud and is one of his earmarks as a writer. In his past books, he has jumped from black militants to Russian Jews to Italian gangsters, written about magic and realism, and has tried everything from stream-of-consciousness to almost scientific prose. Very few contemporary authors have taken such risks with their careers.

"I wanted to see what I could do," Malamud said. "I felt that the nature of talent is difficult to define and that one way of trying to define it is to see what it can do.

"You know, some people felt that *The Fixer* was written out of some compulsion I had to deal with the fate of the Jews. It was a serious novel, but in essence it was, like my other books at the time, somewhat experimental. Can you do this, can you do it well? Those were the major questions I asked myself."

Malamud's books, as wide-ranging as they are, can be roughly divided into two types, the modern-life novels and the Jewish books. The modern-life novels, which are either not about Jews or are about men whose Jewishness is incidental to them, tend to be less believable, lively, or well written than the others. In *The Natural*, for instance, Malamud's first novel, about Roy Hobbs, a baseball star who keeps making the wrong decisions, the gentile protagonist never quite becomes three-dimensional. *A New Life*, his third novel, about an alcoholic college professor who tries and fails to improve his life, is so accurate about academics that it is flat and dull. And *Dubin's Lives*, about a middle-aged biographer who nearly wrecks his marriage by falling for an unprepossessing student half his age, has long sections that stretch credulity to snapping point.

The Jewish books, on the other hand—*The Assistant*, *The Fixer*, *The Tenants*, *Pictures of Fidelman*, and his three volumes of short stories—are more poetic, moving, and humorous than the others. They are also the ones that have won Malamud his awards—two National Book Awards, one for *The Fixer* and one for a book of stories called *The Magic Barrel*, and a Pulitzer prize, also for *The Fixer*. *God's Grace* rates with these better Jewish books, although its flaws, particularly the clichéd chimps, prevent it from reaching the level of his best short stories or of *The Fixer*, his most success-fully executed book. Malamud, however, does not like having his books characterized as Jewish, compliment intended or not.

"Jewishness is important to me, but I don't consider myself only a Jewish writer," he once said in an interview. "I have interests beyond that, and I feel I am writing for all men." In the same interview he added, "All men are Jews, except that they don't know it. I think it's an understandable statement and a metaphoric way of indicating how history, sooner or later, treats all men."[3]

This is certainly true in *God's Grace*. Nuclear war is a holocaust for us all.

Whether he likes it or not, however, Malamud has always been considered one of America's major Jewish writers, along with Saul Bellow and Philip Roth. ("Bellow pokes fun at this sort of thing," he once said, "by calling Bellow-Malamud-Roth the Hart, Shaffner, and Marx of Jewish-American literature.") He has not reached the acclaim of Bellow, because his work has been so uneven in quality, but he is more respectable than Roth, having produced more and avoided stooping to Roth's boyish vulgarity. In writing about *The Assistant* for the *New York Times*, Morris Dickstein explained the Jewishness of Malamud's work. "Malamud had distilled what seemed like the emotional essence of first-generation Eastern Eu-ropean Jews, stoic, self-abnegating, mildly hysterical, passionately familial—all done with a sureness of touch that makes Bellow and Roth seem assimilated, and whose only peer, it seems clear today, is that anachronistic survivor, I. B. Singer."[4]

Malamud is not as immersed in Judaic culture and tradition as Singer, however. He can embrace a Yiddish idiom or leave it, write of the Old World or the New. When he was asked by Israel Shenker to describe a typical Malamudian character for the *New York Times*, he said "A Malamudian character is someone who fears his fate, is caught up in it, yet manages to outrun it. He's the subject and object of laughter and pity."[5]

This describes a character with more hope, more courage, and a little less foolishness than the recurring schlemiel in Singer's works. Yakov Bok, for instance, emerges spiritually triumphant after im-prisonment and torture at the hands of anti-Semites in czarist Russia. But just because Malamud has avoided the archetypal schlemiel does not make his writing any less Jewish. As Dickstein wrote, "Though *The Assistant* and *The Magic Barrel* boast no char-acter like Portnoy or Herzog monomaniacal enough to become a cultural byword, they have claims to being the purest expression of the Jewish imagination in American literature."[6]

Malamud's preoccupation with the question of how humans use their freedom, how they try to "outrun" their fate, is expressed in many of his books through the metaphor of a prison, from its most literal in *The Fixer* to its most abstract—Cohn's solitude on earth. "It is a metaphor for the dilemma of men throughout history," Malamud once explained to critics Leslie and Joyce Field. "Necessity is the primary prison, though the bars are not visible to all. Then there are the man-made prisons of social injustice, apathy, ignorance. There are others, tight or loose, visible or invisible, according to one's predilection or vulnerability."

Malamud's first figurative prison, the grocery store in *The Assistant*, his second novel, came from his own experience. His parents, Russian immigrants who settled in Brooklyn, made their living by running such a store, and after Malamud's mother died when he was fifteen, he had to spend more time than ever confined behind the counter. Anyone who reads his early stories of grocery-store life will never again be able to enter one without feeling guilt and pity.

Malamud first began writing when he was a teenager working in that store—he used to turn his homework into stories—and many of the settings for his fiction since have been drawn from his life. The Brooklyn shopkeepers and Jewish immigrants came from his childhood; the blacks in his stories "The Angel Levine" and "Black Is My Favorite Color" and in *The Tenants* from his days teaching in Harlem when he was thirty-four; the academic life in *A New Life* from his twelve years teaching in Oregon; the material for his Italian stories and *Pictures of Fidelman* from the year he spent in Italy with his wife of Italian background, Ann de Chiara; and finally, the Vermont setting for *Dubin's Lives* from his present home in Bennington, where he has been living and teaching on and off for twenty years.

Although Malamud began writing when he was young, he did not publish in major magazines until he was thirty-six and already married with a son, Paul. This was mainly because much of his twenties were taken up with getting a bachelor's degree from City College in New York and a master's from Columbia University, and with working in such places as factories and stores to support himself. "I had written a few stories in college, [and] after graduation I began to write again," he has explained. "The rise of totalitarianism, the Second World War, and the situation of the Jews in Europe helped me to come to what I wanted to say as a writer."

In 1949, when he was thirty-five, Malamud was offered a job teaching English at Oregon State College in Corvallis; so he left his home in Greenwich Village and moved there with his family. Because he had no doctorate, he was in an insecure position at the college, just as Levin is in *A New Life,* but eventually he earned the position of associate professor. It was in Oregon that his career took off. He published in several major magazines in 1950, and in 1952 his first novel was published and his daughter Janna was born. Four years later, he received a *Partisan Review* fellowship, which he used to go with his family to Italy. "Through my wife's relatives and acquaintances I was almost at once *into* Italian life and got the feel of their speech, modes of behavior, style," Malamud once wrote. "When I go abroad I like to stay in one place as long as possible until I can define its quality."

The Malamud family remained in Oregon until 1961, when Malamud was offered a position teaching in the Division of Language and Literature at Bennington College. Despite his success as an author, he has continued to teach throughout his life, either at Bennington or as a visitor at various other campuses. "I'd advise a young writer to make a living any way he can, rather than depend entirely on writing, . . ." he once said. "So if teaching allows him to earn a certain amount of money and maintain his freedom, by all means let him teach, if he can."[7] Malamud has also traveled a lot around Europe and to the Soviet Union, where he went to research *The Fixer.* His story "Man in the Drawer," from *Rembrandt's Hat,* also comes from this visit.

When *Dubin's Lives* came out in 1979, readers were quick to assume autobiography because it was set in Vermont and was about a man near Malamud's age, but Malamud says he no more than "dipped" his "finger into the autobiographical cream." He denies ever having been an autobiographical writer—no strings of disguised Malamuds are to be found in his works. "In essence, a writer sooner or later becomes almost all the characters in his novel," he said, "but I can't measure how strongly I project myself into a character I'm inventing. I can't insist on it because of the need for distancing myself."

That Malamud will never reveal the autobiographical elements of his fiction is indicative of his privateness. For years at the beginning of his career he refused interviews, and he has always kept his family life well out of the public eye. "I know that ours is supposed to be a confessional age and that much gets said trippingly off the tongue," he said, "but my feeling is that if one tells all about oneself, there's nothing left to tell."

Is this attitude a reflection of Malamud's increasing lack of interest in himself as he grows older? "Unfortunately, I don't find myself less interesting at all!" he said, laughing. "I feel I'm more daring in certain ways and braver than I've been, and even less foolish." Then he added seriously, "I haven't lost my fears, but I'm less fearful about life. I ask far more from it than I have in the past."

Is Malamud so much harder on Cohn than his previous heroes because he expects more from life now? Poor Cohn only gets to "outrun" his fate for a short time, he is denied the triumph of Yakov Bok, and *God's Grace* has a bleaker conclusion than any of Malamud's other books. Is he more pessimistic about humankind's fate than he was when he wrote *The Fixer*?

"Yes, I am more pessimistic than I used to be," Malamud said a little sadly. "I feel that the more the world stays the same, the worse it seems to become. Man seems to be a constant disappointment to himself." He hesitated a moment, then added quietly, "In a sense, blaming man gets you nowhere. But, on the other hand, whom else can you seriously blame?"

MALAMUD COMMENTARY

C ircumstances forced me to break most of my rules to do this profile of Bernard Malamud, which is why it reads more like a combination of review and interview than a traditional portrait. I had been assigned to do it for *Saturday Review*, so that it would coincide with the release of Malamud's new book *God's Grace*. But shortly before I was scheduled to go up to his home in Vermont and interview him, he had a severe heart attack and a bypass operation.

After some question as to whether he would be well enough to be interviewed at all, he kindly agreed to let me question him on the telephone. He asked, however, that I send my questions ahead of time so that he would have the chance to think about them and prepare some accurate answers. This gave the interview a different flavor from normal. It forced me to keep my questions as clear and brief as possible and limited the scope of what I could ask him.

Still, as he put it at the end of our conversation, "I imagine that if we were sitting face to face I might have a lot more to say, but there's something nice about a telephone conversation that sticks to the point."

As I could not describe Malamud, except from photographs, or his surroundings, and had to keep the interview short in order not to tire him, I had to rely on my own reviewerly opinions of his books to flesh out the piece. I read everything he had written—not hard, as I had always been a Malamud fan—and found certain patterns in his books that I thought I could apply to his new one. In order to counterbalance my enthusiasm for his work, I also read his critics and tried to incorporate some of their views into the piece. As a result, the article ended up a combination essay-review rather than a conventional profile.

Malamud, whom I did eventually get a chance to meet in person, was a true gentleman. Polite, considerate, and quietly but earnestly honest, he answered my questions frankly and yet with a challenge. As we warmed up on the phone before I began asking questions, he said, "Tell me something about yourself. Do you write anything other than interviews?" And when I mentioned my own fiction, haltingly, he was encouraging. This quality of interest in the other person, no matter how humble, is, I've found, rare in famous people. Susan Sontag, Isaac Bashevis Singer, Jessica Mitford, and Malamud had it, but none of my other interviewees did.

Malamud also showed himself surprisingly insecure about his work. For a man who had published eleven books, he was touchingly eager to know my opinion of his latest. I said that I thought *God's Grace* very funny.

"Oh," he said, sounding pleased. "I'm glad to hear that because I'm concerned about that particular effect. I want a little laughter in that serious book."

"I thought there was a lot of laughter in it," I replied. "I loved the whole conversation with God at the beginning."

"Well, do you find it gets heavy later on, or do you find that it can take what it has to?" Malamud asked anxiously.

"I found it could take it. It seemed well balanced."

"Oh, thank you!" Malamud said with undisguised pleasure.

Looking back on this conversation, it is particularly poignant, because Malamud did not receive favorable reviews for his book. The *Village Voice* in particular savaged it, but the *New York Times* was also unforgiving about his Disneyish apes. When Malamud died a few months after the publication of *God's Grace*, its reception seemed particularly sad, and to my mind, unjust. If only he had lived on to surmount these criticisms and to witness the end of the Cold War and, perhaps, of his vision of nuclear destruction.

Saturday Review accepted the profile and scheduled it for the September issue, then promptly went bankrupt. The magazine later revived under new ownership, but I was caught in the unpaid middle. I shipped the piece around to several magazines, explaining my position, and eventually found it a home in the *Antioch Review*.

SIX

Intrepid Twosome

■

PHOTOGRAPH © NOUVELLE SAARINEN.

JESSICA MITFORD and ROBERT TREUHAFT

The cream Mercedes slows, turns cautiously down the gravel driveway, and comes to a halt. A small, roundish man with a gleaming bald forehead, glasses, and a black moustache gets out and walks up to the front door of his house. As he mounts the wooden steps, a tall woman in a bright pink pantsuit opens the door and grins. "Hello!"

Bob Treuhaft kisses his wife, Jessica Mitford, on the cheek, walks in, and dumps his briefcase on the floor with a sigh of satisfaction.

"The case is over. The time for appeal ran out at 5:00 P.M.—I had a drink to celebrate. Sorry I'm late."

"Hooray!" Mitford claps her hands together, ducks down, and hops up again, swinging one leg out in glee.

"We've won!"

Jessica Mitford, exaristocrat, excommunist, veteran author, and mistress of the exposé, lives with her lawyer husband and fellow muckraker, Bob Treuhaft, in a brown shingle house in Oakland near the Berkeley line. Their house, set back a few paces from the tree-lined road, exudes a peaceful privacy; plants drape over the balcony and cling to the walls, wooden latticework on the windows discourages intruders. Yet, the couple, sixty-three and sixty-seven, respectively, welcomes guests with generous hospitality.

"Come in, come in," Mitford (known as Decca or Dec by family and friends) says to me after greeting her husband. "What would you like to drink?" Treuhaft disappears upstairs to change out of his lawyer's garb and Mitford ushers me into the living room, where there's a drink on the coffee table next to a pile of papers she's been working on. We sit down; she takes off her glasses to reveal luminous blue eyes and, still grinning with pleasure, explains the victory of the day in an accent so English and upper class that one would never guess she had been in this country for more than forty years.

"Bob's just won an *incredibly* important police brutality case in Oakland," she says excitedly. "I admire him *enormously* for it. The *Tribune* was full of it after he peppered them with letters saying they hadn't been covering it."

Mitford has reason to be excited. She and Treuhaft have a long history of fighting the Oakland police, climaxing in the case of Jerry Newson in 1949. Newson, an eighteen-year-old black shoe-shiner, was accused of murdering a white pharmacist and his assistant in Oakland and was sentenced to death after being found guilty by an all-white jury. "The case had all the classic elements of a police frame-up," Mitford has written. "A forced confession, faked ballistic evidence, police intimidation of Newson's teenaged friends, prosecution collusion with the *Oakland Tribune*, which in headlines virtually pronounced Newson guilty the day he was charged."[1] Treuhaft and his law partner were his volunteer lawyers; Mitford was assigned to track down Newson's alibi witnesses. After days of persistent questioning, she came up with enough evidence to get the jury overturned. The charges were dismissed.

Treuhaft comes in with a glass of sherry, settles himself in a chair opposite his wife, and talks about his latest case.

"The case finished today. It was a killing by the Oakland police of a black man in February of 1975 and it wasn't tried until August of 1980," he says, speaking methodically in a scratchy voice. "Much to our surprise, we won a verdict of $117,500 against the police, and they didn't even try to negotiate a reduction of the settlement. It's the first jury verdict against the police in Alameda County in fifteen years. I think the one fifteen years ago was my case also." He pops a pretzel stick into his mouth and chews contemplatively.

Mitford and Treuhaft have been married for thirty-eight years, yet they seem an odd match. Although Mitford looks like a typical middle-American of advanced age—her short hair is gray, her face round, and her clothes bright and synthetic—she still exudes the type of enthusiastic self-confidence that English schoolgirls are wont to call jolly-hockey-stick-ness. She speaks rapidly in a rich, throaty voice, is warm and friendly, and listens to people with intense concern. Yet, as she talks about her work or her enemies, one quickly discovers the Mitford of the merciless pen, the journalist who exposes corruption with scintillating ridicule and who justifies herself with the ingenuous "I just don't like people who do rotten things."

Treuhaft, however, seems harmless. He is calm, almost plodding, and speaks thoughtfully, taking his glasses on and off repeatedly with a weary, absentminded air as if it would never occur to him to do battle with anyone, let alone the Oakland police. Sometimes he even shuts his eyes in concentration as he talks. Where Mitford shoots out her jokes, he builds up to them, delivering the punch line with kindly pleasure.

"I admire Decca terrifically for the way she tortures various unkind people," their son, Benjamin Treuhaft, tells me later. "I admire my father for his Brooklyn sense of humor."

The couple's backgrounds could hardly be more different either. Treuhaft was brought up in New York, first in the Bronx, then in Brooklyn, the son of Jewish immigrants who pushed him hard into education and success. His mother, a character whom Mitford describes with mischievous delight in her second volume of autobiography, *A Fine Old Conflict*, owned a fancy hat shop on Manhattan's Park Avenue, dreamed of conventional glory for her son, and bewailed his radical ways and peculiar wife.

Mitford, on the other hand, grew up in an atmosphere of cultivated eccentricity. She was raised in the English countryside with five sisters and a brother by her odd parents and a string of governesses, the best of whom taught her to shoplift. She was never even sent to school, so her imagination and rebellious spirit remained unsubdued by the traditional English school fare of prayers, cold baths, and porridge. At an early age she was already rejecting the classist and eventually fascist leanings of her family. In her first autobiography, *Daughters and Rebels*, she describes the dawning of her socialist consciousness, inspired by a visit to the poor in her village.

"I say," she said to her mother, "wouldn't it be a good idea if all the money in England could be divided up equally among everybody? Then there wouldn't be any really poor people."

"It wouldn't be fair, darling," her mother replied. " 'You wouldn't like it if you saved up all your pocket money and Debo spent hers, and I made you give up half your savings to Debo, would you?' I immediately saw the point. My idea was pretty hopeless after all."[2]

Mitford was not to accept such explanations for long. In reaction against the facism of her sisters and parents—Unity became a friend of Hitler, Diana married the head of the British Union of Fascists, and her parents had tea with Hitler—she ran away at age seventeen with Winston Churchill's leftist nephew and the idol of her youth, Esmond Romilly. They fled to Spain, where they worked as news reporters, but their hopes of joining the forces of the Spanish Republic against Franco were dashed when Mitford's family employed government interference to force the young couple out of Spain.

("I didn't believe the stories Dec told me about her family. I thought it was just exaggeration," Treuhaft says with a bemused smile. "It wasn't until 1955 that I met them and saw they were all just as she'd described. The detestable ones were just as detestable and the crazy ones just as crazy.")

Mitford married Romilly in defiance of her family, and the two moved to London's working-class East End, refusing to have anything to do with her family or to take any money from them (and Mitford never has, to this day). There, she had their first child, a girl. At four months old, the baby caught measles, which soon turned to pneumonia, and died. Later, after the couple had moved to America and Mitford was pregnant again (with Constancia, it turned out, who later became known in the family as "Dinky" or "The Donk"), Romilly was killed at war.

Newly widowed and lying in the charity ward of a Washington, D.C., hospital, about to become a single mother, Mitford still couldn't resist an urge to incite rebellion. One of the patients was only rarely able to urinate normally, yet whenever she rang for a bedpan, the nurse would take so long to arrive that the need would pass and the woman would have to be catheterized, "a painful and revolting procedure." Mitford unfolded a vengeful plan to her fellow patients.

"Next time Mrs. —— rings her bell, I'll count to ten. If a nurse hasn't come by then, let's all wet our beds." Sure enough, the nurse didn't come. The women swung into action and met with resounding success. The nurses never ignored the bell again. "It was my first successful effort at organizing for mass action," wrote Mitford in *A Fine Old Conflict*. "I suppose that twenty years later it would have been described as a pee-in."[3]

A few years later, still in Washington, Mitford took a job at a war agency, the Office of Price Administration (OPA), as a "sub-eligible typist." She soon graduated from this ignoble category to an investigator.

"Sometimes I was assigned to work for Bob Treuhaft, an enforcement attorney, among whose many attractions were his slanting, twinkling black eyes, his marvelously funny jokes and his (to me) exotic Bronx idiom and pronunciation," she wrote.[4]

Treuhaft says he was also attracted by accent. "Well, having gone to Harvard, which was totally anglophile, I was prepared to fall for someone who was English!"

For a first date, Treuhaft asked Mitford to help him on an investigation for the OPA. They have been helping each other in their work ever since.

Despite the differences in their upbringing, Mitford and Treuhaft have always agreed politically. After moving to Oakland in 1945, they worked for the Civil Rights Congress together. One of their activities was to "front" for black families wanting to buy houses in the white areas of Oakland. Once, in 1952, Mitford and friends from the Civil Rights Congress held fort in the house of some of their black friends for an entire night, while a mob of about four hundred white neighbors hurled insults and stones. "It was the first time I had witnessed the horrifying sight and sound of a mob in action," Mitford wrote in *A Fine Old Conflict*. "One could almost feel adrenalin (or perhaps it was the blood of Charlemagne) coursing through one's system at this revolting spectacle. Two uniformed sheriff's deputies stood idly by watching the scene."[5]

Treuhaft and Mitford also joined the Communist Party and stood up for their right to remain silent in front of the House Committee on Un-American Activities. Later, disillusioned by the revelations of Stalin's crimes and fragmentation within the Party, they quit the CP. During the times when Mitford was blacklisted and unable to find a job, she helped Treuhaft investigate his cases.

"She was an awfully good investigator," he recalls, "the same talents that make her a good investigative reporter. She could get statements out of a rock."

Nowadays, Mitford still helps Treuhaft by typing for him when his secretary is "on the blink," as Mitford puts it, and he, in return, helps her at home.

"I have never experienced the bitterness many wives tell about the dreadful way their husbands make them do all the housework," Mitford says. "I make *him* do all the housework! Well, I don't make him, he likes doing it. He finds it relaxing to shop and cook."

Mitford works at home, in a study that was added to the back of the house so that "there would never again be a single paper on the dining room table." As she leads me to the study, we pass the dining room table. It is piled high with papers.

"I don't know why I'm like that!" she laughs apologetically.

The walls of her study are covered with photographs and cartoons of her and her family. One is an original Edward Sorel cartoon captioned "Never underestimate the power of a woman," a reference to Mitford's bestseller *The American Way of Death*, in which she exposed the way the funeral industry fleeces the bereaved. The cartoon shows a typewriter with keys spelling her name and an undertaker being rolled through it like a sheet of paper. Mitford says she is still considered a mortal enemy by the trade.

"There was a *frightfully* sad article in *Mortuary Management* [an undertakers' trade journal] about the death rate falling," she tells me. "Apparently it's due to the fifty-five-mile speed limit and to new advances in cancer and heart disease on the medical front. That, with the rise of cremation, which the undertakers call 'Burn and Scatter' or 'Bake and Shake,' is disastrous for the trade. A lot of them have gone under, and they blame me!" She says this in the voice of a wounded innocent, then laughs and sits down on the edge of a couch. Turned halfway toward me and smoking continually, she talks of her successes.

"The fame, such as it was, came with *The American Way of Death*, which was published when I was forty-six. It came very late in life and I was *absolutely* thrilled. There's nothing like being propelled to the top." One of the aspects of fame that especially pleased her was being paid for her writing, something Treuhaft had difficulty adjusting to.

"I must admit it took me some time to become accustomed to the idea of Decca's prominence," he confesses. "First, she had been Lawyer's wife and suddenly I was Author's husband! I never felt any twinges of jealousy or anything, but it took some pounding away to be able to understand that she had felt burdened by my being the breadwinner. Once she did earn money, she was very jealous of it. It did lead to some difficult times."

With Mitford's recognition came the demand for her to make

national lecture tours, something she still vastly enjoys. Speaking about the first promotional tour she did for *The American Way of Death*, she says, "There was this wonderful fellow, Dan Green—he was sort of wet behind the ears, age twenty-four—who was supposed to carry my luggage and look after keys and tickets. Well, he was *hopeless*, half the time he'd lose everything. Now, my dear, he is senior vice-president or something of Simon and Schuster. I always say I put him on the map.

"Anyway, there was one wonderful time when we were in some sort of rather mediocre town, in the Hilton Hotel, and a television crew came to my room at 8:30 A.M. My room was a broom closet, it was literally [she holds up her hands to demonstrate] *tiny*, with a small sort of monk's single bed. The television people said, 'I would have thought Simon and Schuster would have done better for you than this.' It turns out that there was a huge royal suite that I was supposed to have which *Dan* had, probably just by mistake because he was such an idiot."

Mitford now divides her working time between traveling, lecturing, and writing. She occasionally visits England to see friends and one of her three surviving sisters, Debo, the Duchess of Devonshire. "I don't see anything of Diana and haven't except once when Nancy was dying, sort of over the deathbed. Pamela is the unknown Mitford sister and lives in the country with various horses and dogs and chickens. We call her 'Woman' in family circles. She's all right, but I'm not that interested in chickens and horses, so I don't correspond with her much."

At home, Mitford lives a quiet life with occasional visits from her son, Benjamin, a thirty-two-year-old piano tuner in Berkeley, and frequent phone calls to Dinky, an emergency-ward nurse living in Atlanta with two children of her own.

Mitford and Treuhaft had another child, a boy who was killed by a bus while delivering papers when he was eleven. The accident was extremely upsetting for the family, and Mitford never mentions it in her autobiographies.

Having once had children in the house has left its mark on Mitford's habits as a writer. She gets up at about 6:00 A.M., writes for several hours, and then usually meets someone for lunch.

"I think this regime began because I hoped to have an hour or two before the children came clattering down to breakfast. I've always kept to it, although there are long since no children clattering. But if you're up early, there's the totally delusory feeling that you're three hours ahead. In *fact*, you fall straight asleep in the afternoon, or I do," she says in a conspiratorial tone. "I'm very lazy at bottom."

Once she has a draft of her work written, which she says takes her "ages," she shows it to friends and family, especially Treuhaft. "He's a *marvelous* editor. He's got a much better sense of grammar and syntax than I have."

Treuhaft finds this editing somewhat dangerous. "We get into rows occasionally," he admits. "People who say be unsparing in your criticism usually don't mean it!"

Benjamin is also brought in at this stage. "She loves it when you read and start laughing," he says. "She runs into the room and says, 'Why are you laughing?' If you won't say, she says, 'No roaring without telling!' "

Treuhaft also helps her with article and book ideas. He furnished the ideas for *The American Way of Death*, for example, and even helped her write and research it.

"You see, Decca doesn't like research," Treuhaft says. "She won't even go to the library. I did all that and also the fieldwork because she didn't like going into mortuaries either." Mitford wanted Treuhaft's name on the cover with hers, but her editor advised against it. Treuhaft didn't mind accepting a dedication instead.

"She's always been extremely good in giving me more than credit for my participation," he says.

After many years of constantly attending political meetings, demonstrations, and campaigns, Mitford and Treuhaft have cut down their political activities lately.

"I can't find any political niche anymore," Mitford says. "We work for Congressman Dellums and for certain local issues, but it's very small. There's the New American Movement, which many of my friends have joined, but the thought of going to endless meetings discussing strategy and tactics sort of puts me off. Perhaps it's laziness and old age on my part. I feel somehow that I do more by writing about things than by going to meetings."

She adds that the Left is now so fragmented and directionless that she finds it no longer inspiring, even in the face of the New Right. "The New Right is like muggers waiting for you on the street. If you fear to walk outside because of the muggers, then it's bad news. But I'm not sure the New Right is any more frightening than that. When you look around at all the diverse issues, the main enemy is always corporate capitalism."

Nevertheless, she still prefers the communist newspaper *People's World* over the San Francisco papers. "Those papers are *dreadful*. When you get the Sunday *Examiner* with the gloomy face of Hearst right on the front page, I mean it puts you off your breakfast. But I've got a lifetime subscription to the *People's World* which I gained in the late 1940s by oversubscribing my quota. I always feel that when the *People's World* gives out, I'll give out also!"

When she isn't working, Mitford sees friends, reads, plays Scrabble, or watches television. "My favorite program is 'Name That Tune.' It's so *awful*," she says with a delighted giggle. "It combines every one of the worst features of television and I absolutely can't stay away from it. It has these absurd people dancing around being told they're going to get $100,000 if they can name that tune and you see them making *total* buffoons of themselves. When I've missed that, I feel I've missed everything."

Since her last book, *Poison Penmanship: The Gentle Art of Muckraking*, came out in 1979, Mitford has been working on various magazine pieces and giving what she calls "The Speech" (her popular lecture on the funeral industry and muckraking) to audiences throughout the country. She is still in demand as the author of *The American Way of Death* and *Kind and Usual Punishment*, as the muckraker who exposed the Famous Writers' School, and as a wit. With so many accomplishments to her credit, how does she see herself? As a writer, a muckraker, a wife? She takes a deep drag on her cigarette, frowns, and fiddles with her fingers for a minute.

"Oh God, that's hard to answer. I'm often called a muckraker, but that was just a sort of moniker put on me by *Time* magazine. . . . When I'm writing, I'd say, 'Oh, I'm a writer' but now . . . Well, I have a bad leg now and the doctor said I ought to walk a mile a day. I *hate* walking, so I said to my husband, "Well, you know Bob, the average housewife walks five miles a day, so I'm all right.' He said, 'But you're not the average housewife.' " She shifts on the couch, crosses a leg, and looks at me helplessly. "I don't know what I am!"

MITFORD COMMENTARY

Writing a profile of a couple, rather than of one person, has certain advantages. True, one has less space to devote to each individual, but the form allows for an automatic check point. What one person says can be checked with the other, and vice versa. It helps the writer break away from one point of view.

I had a lot of fun with this interview. I was, of course, nervous at first, not only because interviewing a master interviewer makes one feel self-conscious and bumbling but because I had long admired Mitford from afar, and had read everything she'd written before having any idea I would meet her. But Mitford was so welcoming that my nerves quickly passed. Nevertheless, she is a somewhat overpowering character, and I had to work hard not to let her wrest the piece away from me. I now think my admiration may have prevented me from being as clear-sighted as I might have been.

My first decision was to interview the principal characters—Mitford, Treuhaft, and their son, Benjy—separately (Mitford's daughter lived in another state, so I decided to go for the in-person interviews only. Now I would never dream of leaving her out.) I took this approach because in group interviews the interviewees are always restraining themselves or playing up to one another. Also, by talking to Mitford and Treuhaft separately, I could ask them to comment on each other.

The most difficult moment in my research for this piece was when Benjy, their son, told me about the death of his older brother. We were sitting at my kitchen table in Berkeley, the sun pouring in and Benjy's vast dog waiting outside, when he told me that his brother had been killed and that he thought the family had never completely recovered from the death. That statement, plus the fact that I had never seen any mention of this tragedy in print even though Mitford had written two volumes of autobiography, suggested that it was not a subject I could tactfully bring up with her. What should I do? I didn't want to cause her undeserved pain, but at the same time I didn't see how I could leave out such an important part of her life. Eventually, I decided to ask Treuhaft permission to include the information in my article—my instincts told me he was more approachable on the subject—and he granted it. I chose not to make much of the sad story in the article, but I did want to point out that she had lost two of her four children, as well as her first, much-adored husband; that she had experienced a lot of tragedy for one person, and that she nevertheless battled on.

Some journalists would not agree with the approach I took on this delicate matter. I had uncovered a scoop, on record, and many would have run with it without bothering to stop for permission.

But I don't happen to believe authors deserve the same kind of exposé treatment as politicians or wrongdoers, unless they are hypocrites or poseurs.

This subject brings up a vital ethical question about profiles: can one write an accurate and honest profile while knowingly leaving out certain private facts? Tom Wolfe would say no. Referring to journalists who become concerned with the feelings and privacy of their subjects, he wrote, "People who become overly sensitive on this score should never take up the new style of journalism. They inevitably turn out second-rate work, biased in such banal ways that they embarrass even the subject they think they are 'protecting.' "[6] I question this statement. A lot of reporters, Tom Wolfe among them, like to pose as tough, stop-at-nothing types who will do anything to get a good story. "To hell with sensitivity," they cry. "To hell with ethics!" Even Mitford herself laughed at ethics in the introduction to *Poison Penmanship*, although in her case with more justification, since she specializes in exposing wrongdoing. But I think a lot of this posturing is just that—a kind of retrospective justification of the voyeurism journalists indulge in, coupled with a lot of showing off. I see no reason why reporters can't bring to certain stories some of the sensitivity they would to a social situation, with the idea that there is no point hurting someone who doesn't deserve it. Being considerate in this way is not a popular idea with news editors and reporters, but I maintain that reporters who don't have this sensitivity, who lack tact, end up losing the trust of their sources and getting less of a story than those who tread gently.

Even though I chose to be tactful where the children were concerned, there were other subjects in this profile that I was less shy of. Both Mitford and Treuhaft have made much of rejecting riches and capitalism throughout their lives, especially, of course, when they were members of the Communist Party, and this made me feel justified in mentioning the cream Mercedes. Indeed, I felt compelled to mention it, for I was surprised at their having such an ostentatious car. I also turned Mitford's "Queen of the Muckraker" techniques on her a little and asked them what they live on and whether it was true that she has never accepted a penny from her family since she left home.

Since this profile was published, in 1981, Benjy has married, *Poison Penmanship* has been reprinted, and Mitford has come out with another, lighter book, called *Grace Had an English Heart*. She

still goes on the lecture circuit, she still writes the occasional comment on some current affair, and she is as mocking, barbed, and
wicked as ever. She is now, she recently told me, working on an
exposé about maternity hospitals and the poor. As she put it, "It's
a sort of 'American Way of Birth.' "

SEVEN

A Talk with

■

PHOTOGRAPH © 1981, THOMAS VICTOR.

LEONARD MICHAELS

On a sunny Thursday afternoon in Berkeley, inside a white house protected by pale green shutters, a faded picket fence, and a tangle of California plants, Leonard Michaels helps his sixteen-month-old daughter down the stairs.

"Come on baby, you can do it." At the bottom she begins to cry. He picks her up, remarking with rueful pride that she senses he is about to leave, and nuzzles her weeping face affectionately. In a New York drawl that is almost a snarl, he speaks in baby talk: "Where is my nose? Where is my eye? Where is my hair?" Then he hands his child to the baby sitter and carefully sneaks out of his front door and around to his study in the basement. "If she thinks I'm still home," he explains, "she'll cry for me."

Michaels is a professor of English literature at the University of California in Berkeley and the father of three children. He lives in a large house in the hills and divides his time between teaching, writing, and fighting what he calls "the homeowner's war against chaos." In this setting, it is hard to recognize him as the creator of Phillip Liebowitz, the protagonist of the story collections *Going Places* and *I Would Have Saved Them If I Could* who writhed with lovers on taxicab floors, dissected his friends with eloquent cynicism, and mocked his Jewish family with vicious wit.

"I think I'll probably never return to Phillip," Michaels says in his cool dark basement study. "I think he's finished, gone, of no interest to me anymore. And I think it's too bad."

Sitting sideways at his desk, leaning on his elbow, his legs casually sprawled out, he talks slowly and cautiously between deep drags on his cigarette.

"Phillip represented a certain kind of spirit and attitude toward experience which I really had to get beyond. Sometimes I feel a kind of regret that I no longer want to write that way—it was too young. That time was a lot crazier in its passions than now."

Michaels's latest work, *The Men's Club*, is about a group of men in early middle age who get together in a Berkeley house for a night and swap tales. The sexual athlete Liebowitz has been replaced by men who are burdened with families, careers, and domestic feelings. As the men relax into intimacy, they begin to reminisce about their wilder pasts while simultaneously vandalizing the house in which they hold their meeting. Are these men in some kind of midlife crisis, reverting to boyhood as a sign of nostalgia for their youth? Michaels grimaces at the question: "I'm not sure what a midlife crisis is. Personally, I've lived in a state of crisis for about twenty years." The grimace turns to a smile.

"As for the men in my novel, they are not so much thinking about midlife crisis as about the fact that they have lived long enough to see that things tend to happen to them in a particular way, in a pattern that is deeply personal. Yet they ask: could this be me? In the group, they say things about themselves they wouldn't have said otherwise, and they learn about themselves this way. But just as important, they listen to the others, and each of them learns how much he is like the others.

"I'll give you a midlife example. Recently, at a dinner party in New York, I was introduced to a certain writer. I said: 'Glad to meet you.' He said: 'We've met.' I said: 'No, I don't think so.' He shouted: 'Yeah, yeah, yeah, we've met!' Everyone stopped talking and stared at us, waiting for the truth to emerge—it was a New York crowd, hungry for truth. But our host said: 'Okay, let's eat.' So everyone began eating and I never found out why that man thinks we met. Perhaps he thought he *was* me. Maybe, at some point in your life, you meet yourself. Maybe that's a midlife crisis. If so, it describes the men in my novel."

At forty-seven, Leonard Michaels looks as if he has lived through a lot. His dark curly hair, tumbled about as if never quite controllable, has tinges of gray, and his face is olive-skinned and rough, with deep lines running from his nose to his thin mouth. When he is thinking, he furrows his thick brows over deep-set eyes and appears either bored or in pain. Yet he has a street-corner grace.

One can imagine him dribbling a basketball (a game he played with fanatical zeal as a youth in New York) with fierce concentration across a city parking lot, his thin frame effortlessly dodging and bending around an obstacle course of cars. He still takes possession of a chair with the cool, easy confidence of an athlete. This afternoon, in his basement study, he seems equally confident talking about *The Men's Club*, his first published novel. He calls it a "descent into the human."

"By that I mean that the considerations of literary art in this book are supposed to seem minimal. Everything I talk about, I try to talk about in regard to human reality, which is a much sloppier thing than art. There are no questions of form in life itself. People do what they are compelled to do and react the way they must."

The desire to be guided by reality rather than by a notion of art is what Michaels says finally enabled him to write a novel. He twice before tried novels, but because of the "severe" ideas he then held about a writer's obligation to art, neither came to fruition. The first, which he wrote as a graduate student, he incinerated. The second turned into the staccato series of short stories in his collection *I Would Have Saved Them If I Could*.

"My stories were very much intended to be true to a kind of musical destiny, almost like poems," he says, leaning dangerously far back in his chair and looking pensive. "There's a story called 'Hello Jack' which I'm very fond of because it's written in a kind of New York music. But I think I've gotten beyond that now. No reader can suppose that I was obsessed with the look and sounds of words in the novel the way I was in my stories. I was careful about that: I reread the novel many times and whenever I'd spot a passage that was too well written, I'd mess it up."

Nevertheless, Michaels has not relinquished his concern with rhythm in his writing. He calls himself a "very physical writer," who feels the beat of his language unconsciously ("If my nerves go wrong, the writing goes wrong"); yet he considers the beat essential. "The beat is supposed to give you the feeling of lived time, or the quality of the tension in these men during the long night they spend together," he says emphatically.

The subject of the novel was inspired by a visit Michaels paid to an actual men's group in Berkeley. As in the novel, he was invited along by a friend. At first he resisted: "The men I know in New York would laugh at the idea! It's too artificially personal, the California version of sincerity. In a group like that you deliberately make yourself vulnerable, open to the scrutiny of the others in the room—as if your psychological life could be put on exhibit like a collection of stamps. In California there tends to be less difference between interior and exterior realities. Houses are built with big windows so the outside world and the inside world flow together, which is confusing for birds. They go crashing into the windows and get killed. But I think people in New York are more protective of their interior lives. Maybe they already feel vulnerable enough. A ride in the subway can be more intensely personal than a year in a Berkeley men's group."

Still, Michaels allowed himself to be persuaded to go, however reluctantly: "I was working hard at school and had all kinds of domestic businesses and complications that created hours and hours of tension. And I was simply lonely. But I didn't go expecting anything like relief from my loneliness. I expected to be an observer. I went very cynically, ready for all kinds of silliness."

Given these prejudices, he found himself surprisingly moved by the group. The men met periodically for a year, and at each meeting one would tell of his life and troubles. "Meeting after meeting, I found myself profoundly concerned about the unhappiness of a man whom I hardly knew," Michaels says, still with some wonder. But he chose to leave out of his novel the actual men he met and much of their tragedy. To use their stories, he says, would have felt like gossip, not writing.

"The group of men in my novel will not allow misery to just sit there in the room," he says. "They're going to chip away at it and convert it to humor one way or another. There's something about the fact that it's a group of men talking which makes for a kind of happiness, even if the stories are downers."

Most of the stories are about failure in love, friendship, communication, and hope. Several of them are willed failures, deliberate sabotages of possible happiness. "I think it's true in life too," Michaels says, swiveling around in his chair to reach for another cigarette. "A lot of failure one notices isn't because fate has led to it, it's just what people damn well want. I once picked up a woman hitchhiker in Berkeley, and before we'd driven a block, she told me that the last time she hitched, she'd been raped. I asked her if she hitched frequently. She said, 'Of course.' Then she started telling me she had a right to do whatever she wants, she's a free person. The more she talked, the angrier she got, and suddenly she told me to get rid of my filthy cigarette, then flung open the door and jumped out. That woman was a complete failure as a hitchhiker.

"Maybe people prefer failure to the possibility of success because they see success as a kind of death. They would much rather be in a condition of failure and depression and anguish—at least they know they're alive!" he says with a laugh.

Leonard Michaels never intended to write about his men's group until an editor at *Cosmopolitan* magazine asked for an article. He proposed a piece on the men's group. By the time he finished it, he knew he did not have anything for *Cosmopolitan*, but he did have the beginnings of a novel. "When I realized I had a novel on my hands, I got pretty excited," he says, though he rarely shows excitement. "The novel emerged much the way my stories do, by a certain kind of luck."

He took two and a half years to finish the novel, with all the traveling, teaching, and lecturing he was doing, but the actual writing time was only six or seven months. He describes it as "a horrible agony."

"I have the worst possible habits as a writer. I can't write page two until I'm satisfied with page one, so I rewrite page one twenty-five times, then page two, and meanwhile I'm dying to get to page thirty. What I publish is usually pretty thin and ecologically sound, but the paper I waste getting to it is equivalent to a small forest."

He also had his moments of despair, especially when he was trying to write about experiences generally inaccessible to fiction. "Even if I knew the experience well and could talk about it easily with friends, when I tried to write about it I'd lose heart and think, 'It can't be done.' It's real, but there was no way, I thought, to make it seem real. Then I learned that if I waited, the book would reach a point where it allowed that sort of thing to be said. One of the most remarkable experiences I had in writing the book was that I learned a kind of patience."

Michaels writes at home in an austere study that is designed to provide privacy rather than comfort. There is a narrow bookcase, a small rug, and one dingy art poster on the wall, but otherwise the room is virtually bare, except for the desk that faces a blank wall. The window beside his twenty-two-year-old Olivetti looks out onto shrubbery, without a glimpse of the dazzling view of San Francisco Bay visible from the rest of the house.

During the periods when he is writing, he reads philosophy—

Hegel, Marx, Nietzsche, Plato—but never fiction, toward which he feels a temporary generalized revulsion. His favorite short story writers are Franz Kafka, Flannery O'Connor, Isaac Babel, and James Joyce, but even these he will not touch: "It's so contagious, you don't even know it's happening sometimes. You pick up the peculiar rhythm of another writer, or you find yourself playing with attitudes you discover in some other novelist that are not yours at all. I don't want to be subjected to that kind of temptation when I write."

Leonard Michaels did not begin writing fiction until he was a graduate student at the University of Michigan. His first reader and critic was his roommate: "He read everything I wrote. He even listened to my typing. An extremely competitive guy. If he said one of my stories was good, I'd know it was bad. If he looked depressed, I'd know it was good."

He was published in literary magazines almost immediately, and started winning prizes and getting invitations to read. This was a mixed blessing. "I received the kind of attention that made it more difficult to write," he says with a slightly sad grin, "but I think I've been very lucky. Almost everything I've wanted to publish has been published."

In spite of his early success, he decided that he could never make a living at writing, so he completed his Ph.D. and took a teaching post. He says that a regular salary check has always been essential to his writing and his peace of mind.

He chose to teach at Berkeley in order to be as far as possible from New York City, where he grew up, the son of Jewish immigrants. He visits New York frequently, on business or to see his friends and family, but can hardly bear the place for longer than two weeks and does not even like to talk about it. "I'm a New Yorker still, but I don't miss New York," he says bluntly. He has been in Berkeley for thirteen years and plans to stay.

At Berkeley, he teaches literature and at least one writing course a year. "I want to do it. It has important gratifications for me, though I'm aware of the dangers," he says. "For example, while I'm discussing a student's work, or trying to analyze why something fails or succeeds, I begin to reveal certain things to myself that are best kept hidden. Personal things. Intuitions about style, dramatic effects, the way a story can mean this or that. All these intuitions ought to remain on the level of instinct or feeling. Even if they aren't exactly hidden from yourself, they somehow lose their energy when you articulate them. It's rather like the poem by William Blake: 'Never seek to tell thy love / Love that never told can be.' "

Ideally, Michaels would like to be free of other obligations while he is writing, "but this is something I've never had in my life!" he laughs. "What I have had are two or three days at a time with few interruptions. I'm a streak shooter. Five shots in a row, then nothing for the rest of the game. I live for miracles. All my writing is done at home. If the phone rings, I answer it. When the mail arrives, I read it. An old friend hits town and I'll go out to dinner with him. My kids go banging around the house. Some writers complain about how life has cheated them of the time to write, but I suspect we get more time than we deserve in America. Babel and Mandelstam didn't get nearly enough in Russia. Flannery O'Connor died much too young. Kafka didn't live very long and he didn't want to live even that long, yet no modern writer has equaled his achievement. Years ago, I received a Guggenheim Fellowship. I asked for six months because I felt too ashamed to ask for more."

Michaels says his main ambitions are to write one more novel and to be thought of as a good writer. "I'd like to be thought of as a writer who, for better or worse, never sold out, never compromised his own notions of what serious writing entails," he says thoughtfully. He stops a moment, takes a last drag on a cigarette, holds his breath while slowly grinding out his cigarette in the ashtray, then suddenly lets the smoke out of his lungs.

"I'm always surprised to see how my work is understood from the outside," he continues. "Recently I found a book of mine selling in a rare book store for an enormous amount of money. It was like being presented to myself as dead." A sardonic grin appears.

"Maybe that's an honor, being good enough to be considered dead."

MICHAELS COMMENTARY

Of all the profiles I've done, this was the most looked over, edited, controlled, and watched. Leonard Michaels wanted to perfect his spoken words as much as his written ones, especially for the *New York Times* audience, so we struck a deal. I would interview him, transcribe the interview, and let him see the transcript. He would rewrite his answers, polish them but keep them to my points. I would then write the piece as I saw fit, using the polished quotations.

That deal made me uneasy enough, but once the piece reached the *Times* editor, it went through still more interference. Unbeknownst to me, the editor showed—or at least read—the piece to Michaels, an act that went against my ethical standards. In fact, the piece suffered very little change as a result of this—when I compare my manuscript to the printed version, they are virtually identical. But Michaels did make one complaint: when my editor read my description of him, which at the time read, "Yet, he has a street-corner grace. One could imagine him slipping noiselessly along dark walls, or dribbling a basketball with fierce concentration across a parking lot, his thin frame dodging and bending effortlessly," Michaels's comment was, "She makes me sound like a rat!" The "slipping noiselessly" therefore got expunged.

Michaels, or "Lenny," as he is usually known, had been a professor of mine at Berkeley, from whom I had taken writing and literature courses when I was a graduate student. When I heard he had a new book coming out, his first novel, I saw the opportunity to approach the *New York Times Book Review* with the suggestion of a profile. Being his former student and being right there in Berkeley might, I reckoned, give me an edge over my competitors.

Having no connection with the *Times*, I wrote my query carefully, making sure to put in my own observations of Michaels's uniqueness and character, and to make it clear that I had read and knew his work. I also let them know that I had already read the novel in manuscript, a copy of which Michaels had given me. To my delight, I was assigned the piece. Later, I discovered that one of my friends, also a student of Michaels, had been given an assignment from the *Times* to do the same thing. The *Times* has since sworn that the duplication was an accident, a result of each editor acting relatively independently, but at the time it was awkward for my friend and me. Meanwhile, Michaels granted interviews to both of us and waited, as did we, to see which would be picked.

My interview with Michaels was tense but productive. He was extremely anxious about how his book was to be received and how he was going to be presented to the public. I remember meeting him in a café one night to pick up his rewritten questions. He sat, taut and electric with anxiety over his espresso, showing me the pages he had painstakingly typed out. On every page several lines were crossed out in heavy black ink, ensuring I would be utterly unable to decipher the rejected words. He clearly approached his interview as he did his fiction—with obsessive rewriting.

The piece was run with a front-page review of his novel *The Men's Club*. It was more of an interview-plus-description than a true profile because it was designed to go along with the review of his book and because it was intended for the *Times Book Review* audience. Rereading the interview now, I think the independent, rounded-off quality of the quotations shows. The interview, although an accurate depiction of what Michaels is like, does not have the spontaneity of true conversation, and were I to receive such an assignment now, I would not agree to let him rewrite his quotations. I don't mind checking quotations with the source to ensure accuracy, as I did with Sontag, but I don't think journalists should allow themselves to be made into publicity agents. With profiles, that is always a danger.

EIGHT

A Day in the Life
of an Unknown Poet

■

DRAWING © 1990 STEPHEN O'CONNOR

BERTRAND BARD

've lost my specs—can you hold on a moment? This is an emergency. I *must* find my specs."

The poet Bertrand Bard* is beginning his poetry reading at 4:00 this Tuesday afternoon at UC Berkeley. He has flown over from London and then up from Los Angeles for the purpose.

It is now 4:10. I can see his wild red hair and moth-eaten ginger beard bent earnestly over the telephone. He is speaking to New York. "George? Yes, it's Bertrand here. Terribly sorry to bother you. . . ." His voice has the drawl of a well-brought-up Englishman, upper class, Oxford education. The drawl is hauntingly melodious.

"Don't know *what* I've done with them. Pop them in an envelope if you find them, would you?"

He hangs up, and I start forward to take his arm and lead him, forcibly if needs be, to the audience that must be growing impatient in the lecture hall below.

But no. He shoots me a grin, waves one arm, and starts to dial again. I look desperately at the clock. This time it's Miami, and the school secretaries are beginning to look uncomfortable at this extravagant use of their office phone. The poet's spare pair of glasses, rimmed in brown plastic horn, catch the sunlight from the window and gleam. He looks like a sleepy, unshaven mole.

Finally, at 4:15, Bertrand Bard is ready to accompany me to the lecture hall where he is to give his poetry reading, one of many he

*I have changed the poet's name to avoid offense—HB.

129

is touring the country to give this month. Talking rapidly, he apologizes for the delay and bustles over to a corner of the office where he has left an enormous leather bag, spilling over with clothes and papers, and a large package done up in brown paper and string. Still talking, he slings the bag's strap over one scrawny shoulder, picks up the package, and lopes off down the hall in the wrong direction.

I call him back and he swivels, unperturbed, and follows me.

"What other poets have you had reading here?" he asks, plainly excited at the prospect of his own performance.

I name a few big names and look at him curiously. I have heard that he has written to every English professor in the department, asking them to come to his reading. He has also sent them elaborate materials advertising himself as an "exciting performer" and, since his arrival in the country, has phoned most of them. No one here apparently has ever heard of him, let alone read his stuff.

Before we have even reached the staircase, the poet has asked me if I have a car, and could I drive him to the airport after the reading? I am taken aback at being asked such a favor within so few minutes of meeting the man but nevertheless feel guilty when I can't oblige. I ask him if the university has made arrangements for him.

"No, but never mind," he says with a grin. "Maybe someone in the audience will take me."

We arrive at the lecture hall at last, and rush through the door, preparing to apologize to an impatiently buzzing audience.

The poet stops dead halfway inside the room, his body still tilted slightly forward from the impetus of his rushing gait.

There are only five people in the room. Not one of them is a professor.

Feeling· terrible, I introduce the poet and sit down. He looks around, then says "Oh, the usual turnout I see." But, in an instant, he is jovial again. One gets the feeling he is used to such insults.

He tosses the leather bag on the floor, and asks if anyone has a knife. The audience sits, stunned at this apparition, while he begins to tear at the brown package with his fingernails.

This is when I really begin to notice what he looks like. His face, pointed beneath his untrimmed beard, large nosed, is weatherbeaten, lined, and of a yellowish hue. His bright paisley shirt is plainly dirty, and below his very old yellow-green corduroy trousers are a pair of startlingly unmatched socks. One is bright yellow, the other orange.

After he has scattered string and bits of cardboard all over the floor around him, releasing ten copies of his home-printed poetry books, which none of us will be able to afford, he goes over to the double doors and begins a strange, ritualistic fight with them. Again, we sit in silence, watching him for some time before we realize what he is doing.

"How on earth," he pants, "do you get these damn things closed?"

One of the young men gets up and gently lifts a lever. The doors swing shut.

At last the poet sits down, and we begin to relax for the first time. But, in a moment, he is up again, dragging his chair, his bag, his box to the window. This means we all have to get up to drag our chairs to the window, too. We form a semicircle in front of him. He flings open the window, takes a deep breath, and sits down at last.

"Well, you faithful few," he beams at us, "any of you poets?" One fresh-faced young man timidly raises his hand.

"Jolly good," says the poet. He turns to his leather bag, and rummaging through pink pajamas and spare pairs of underwear, brings out a black rubber object in a plastic bag. We watch in some alarm but soon realize it is only a kazoo in the shape of a hunting horn.

"I want to take poetry back to the days of minstrels and lyres," Bard explains. And with that he gives an almighty toot on his horn that makes us all jump out of our seats.

"First my Growing Up poems."

Then in a flurry of words, spoken or sung in a high pitch, accompanied by wildly waving arms, frequent toots of the horn, and rapid stamping of the feet, Bertrand Bard begins to read his poetry.

At first, all we can do is sit, horror-stricken and embarrassed. The poetry is very bad, a mixture of nursery rhymes and verses gleaned from Chaucer. But gradually, the wild performance begins to charm us. The poet remains sitting in his little chair the entire time, but somehow manages to transform it into a stage.

Finally, the poem climaxes with the word "Mummy," that echoes pathetically away into the back of the empty room, and after a small pause, we burst into spontaneous applause at the sheer energy of the performance. The poet grins.

Next come his "Nature Poems," many of which he reads to the

tree outside the window by sticking his head out periodically. This means we miss most of the words, but we clap politely anyway. Then come his love poems, written, he tells us in a tender whisper, for his wife.

I am astonished to learn he has a wife. I had imagined him rather living in a tree with an owl or a rabbit for company.

The love poems, centered on warm pairs of various limbs and appendages, are also very bad. Perhaps sensing this, Bard announces his concluding poem, dedicated to Berkeley itself.

With a flourish of his horn, he begins.

"The," a long toot of the horn, "Day," another toot, "A" toot, "Group of" toot, "Berkeley" toot, "Radicals" a very long toot with several changes of tone, "Were" toot, "Swept" toot, "Away" toot, "On" toot, "The" toot, "Horns" toot, "Of" toot, "A" toot, "MOOSE!"

Once again, he has caught us by surprise. We sit in astonished silence, and he looks at us anxiously.

"Moose—that's right, isn't it? They do have big horns, don't they?"

We assure him he is right, and realize that he probably made up the poem as he went along, each toot of his horn providing him with a moment's time for inspiration. The silence in the room is ominous—we are waiting with some terror to see what he will do next.

But the reading is over. He gets up and begins to repack his unsold books, and his horn.

We applaud for the last time, and, one by one, we sheepishly file out of the room, trying to cover up our eagerness to get away— from this unheard-of poet—and from our guilt at leaving him alone, a rejected salesman, preparing to make his solitary way to the next town, to try and sell himself again.

BARD COMMENTARY

I include this vignette not because it is a great example of journalism, but because it illustrates a different, more unconventional form of profile than do my other pieces. It is part review, part portrait, written after only the one meeting described and based on nothing but gossip, letters, and observation—not a single interview.

The story originated with Leonard Michaels, profiled earlier, when I was his student. He had been receiving letters from Bard for weeks and had been collecting stories from his colleagues about the way the poet pushed himself on people and asked outrageous favors. Michaels became intrigued and assigned his class of creative writing students to attend the reading and write anything they wished based on the fellow and on Michaels's information. It could be pure fiction—we could have the poet enter the room on wings, if we wished—but we were to start by seeing him in person. I hate to think how small the audience would have been if Michaels hadn't given us that assignment!

I wrote two pieces based on Bard, one a rather clumsy fictional rendering of his biography (as I imagined it), the other the piece here, which I showed to Michaels and my journalism professors. To my surprise, my teachers loved it, and the next thing I knew it had been bought by the *San Francisco Examiner* to run in their Sunday magazine, *California Living*.

Now I must admit to having had qualms about this piece. I had not written it with publication in mind but only as a spontaneous exercise, and so I had not taken a great deal of care to check the accuracy of my observations—the exact color of Bard's clothes, for example, or even the exact wording of his quotations. Also, I had not interviewed him nor warned him that I would be writing anything. So I went to my professors with these dilemmas and asked if I shouldn't at least change his name. Their verdict was no: he had given a public performance, so must take the consequences of being reviewed, they said. Somewhat uneasily, I complied.

The *Examiner* published the piece under a title that I, being fresh from England, literally did not understand: "Bombing Benignly in Berkeley." "What's 'bombing' mean?" I asked a friend. I've hated the title ever since. Even more unfortunately, Bard's sister turned out to live in San Francisco and sent the piece to him in England— where, in fact, he is a known poet. He wrote a wildly furious letter to Michaels, in bright red felt pen, if I remember right, complaining that the piece was offensive and unfair in every way, and that not even the colors of his mismatched socks had been rendered accurately.

Every other year or so, I read this piece to my students—keeping my authorship anonymous so they will feel free to criticize it (although they probably guess). The piece always elicits fascinating and angry discussions on ethics, which is why I keep reading it to them. Usually, half the class finds it funny and honest and refreshing, while the other half finds it mean-spirited, unethical, and exploitative. I am somewhere in between. If writers can't ever be honest about their impressions, can't stretch reality a little for the fun of a metaphor (my comment about Bard living in a tree, for example, and his moth-eaten beard), where is the joy in writing? Yet, there is the obligation to be accurate. If I were to do the piece now, I'd take better notes and get the color of his socks right. But I would still have him in the tree, rabbit, owl, and all.

NINE

Never Insult
a Yiddish Typewriter

■

PHOTOGRAPH © 1978 THOMAS VICTOR.

ISAAC BASHEVIS SINGER

first saw Isaac Bashevis Singer four months before he won the 1978 Nobel Prize for Literature, when he was in Berkeley, California to teach at a writer's conference. He was at a party held for the opening of the conference, and struck me as looking frail and much older than his seventy-four years. Later, I came to recognize in him a subtle strength and quickness. As his nine days in Berkeley passed, I grew to respect his wisdom and wit, and, like many before me, became captivated by his Old World courtesy: he sat for hours in a bookstore, neither eating nor drinking, signing book after book with painstaking, individual inscriptions; he shook hands with everyone he met and asked the person's name; and he made time for anyone who wished to see him, regardless of his fatigue and failing health.

The next time I saw him was in New York, six months after he had won the prize, where he was engaged in a public dialogue with Rabbi William Berkowitz at a West Side synagogue. By then I had recovered from my initial awe of Singer. In Berkeley I had wondered who could not admire this man, with his twinkling eyes, rolling Yiddish accent, and upside-down phrases? Who could fail to be amused and impressed by his funny stories—the anecdotes he uses to illustrate his points—and by the learning he shows in his speech? But since then I had read Singer's critics, many of them

PUBLISHED, in various forms, in the *San Francisco Review of Books*, 1978, *California Living*, 1979, *New Wings*, 1979, and *Writer's Digest*, 1980.

his fellow Yiddish writers, who were impervious to these charms. Some had attacked him personally, claiming that his persona of the Jewish writer who believes in imps is an act and that his writing is popular only because it panders to public craving for sex and violence. Others had attacked him as a writer, saying that his Yiddish is clumsy and his stories nothing better than distorted folktales. Many had objected that, by not writing accurately of Jews, Singer has betrayed the memory of an extinct culture. So, I became interested in how Singer, as a Polish Jew and a writer from a murdered culture in a dying language, feels about his responsibility to his people.

"Sometimes I feel that our people, the living and the dead, call me from all sides to do justice to their great lives and unusual deaths," he said in a 1972 interview. "I get up every morning with the feeling of excitement of a man who must do more than is in his power. . . . I would not call myself the last Yiddish writer, but I am certainly one of the last. It is both a tragedy and a responsibility."[1]

Singer's critics say that he has not lived up to this responsibility.

Rabbi Berkowitz at the B'nai Jeshurun Synagogue was also interested in the question of Singer's responsibility as a Jew and a Yiddish writer. As he challenged Singer in front of an audience of almost five thousand, I became aware of a Singer I had not seen before—a rebel and a loner who not only has lost the people and culture of his youth and of his writing but has rejected and been rejected by the remainder of that culture.

With these discoveries fresh in my mind, I went to see him the next night in a hotel room where he and his wife were hiding from reporters. He was exhausted from four weeks of nonstop publicity since the Nobel prize was announced, and lay on a couch during our entire conversation. Here again was a different Singer—no longer the fragile sage of Berkeley, and no longer the entertaining, slightly defiant performer of the night before. He was still as charming, courteous, and attentive as ever, and he still showed the same curiosity about me that he shows everyone he meets, but this time I saw in him a certain bitterness, a trickiness, and above all, an indifference to his public, his critics, and his flatterers. I could see that his wit had become polished and automatic through his being interviewed countless times, and that he had a knack of twisting questions around to fit his pretested answers. I could see that the world takes Singer too literally, and that his public image of an absentminded, superstitious Jew who believes that God rules the universe and that imps hide his glasses is only a small part of the real Singer. And I could see that, although he likes to perform, to charm, to get a laugh, he likes better to write. For this, he wants to be alone.

Singer arrived late at the writers' conference party in Berkeley, tired after his plane journey from New York, where he lives when he is not wintering in Florida. When he walked in, no one took much notice of him. Most of the students were too busy talking to the other, at the time more popular writers in the room, such as William Gaddis and Peter Matthiessen. Several confessed to me that they had never heard of Isaac Bashevis Singer.

Singer looks unhealthy. He is small, stooped, and bald, except for a little wispy white hair, and so thin that the dark suits he always wears seem to dangle off his tiny frame like washing off a hanger. His face, creased in soft lines, is round and very pale. But he says he has always looked unhealthy, even as a young man. "I look emaciated, as if from consumption, pale, and like someone who has just narrowly escaped death," he wrote in one of his autobiographies, *A Young Man in Search of Love.* My impression of his frailty was belied by the alert movement of his eyes and the eager bounce of his step.

As he sat down at a table, I approached him. He immediately stood up again, shook my hand, and asked my name. I told him that, although I wasn't a conference student and hadn't paid any tuition, I would like to see him sometime. He waved a hand. "Eh, I don't care about these rules. They tell me I should do this, I should do that, but this has nothing to do with what I really do. Come anytime." Just then, about four or five elderly women, who had at last spotted Singer, descended on him eagerly. He did not look displeased—he has always, he told me later, been one for the ladies. "I began to think about writing at twelve and about girls at fourteen. These are the two greatest passions of my life."

The next day, armed with a tape recorder, I went to see Singer in his room at the University Faculty Club. "Come in," he said kindly, opening the door for me. I noticed a copy of Irving Howe's *World of Our Fathers* lying on the neatly made bed and a note pad covered with Yiddish scribbles on the bedside table. Ushering me to a chair by the window, he explained, "I was just now sitting down and writing topics and themes. The only thing is, I lose them. Sometimes I find them two years later."

He lowered himself cautiously into an armchair and asked what he could do for me. I was not at all sure if he remembered me, and even after I reminded him I still wasn't sure, even though he nodded and said, "Yes, yes." In the days to follow I often found it hard to tell what he remembered and what he didn't. He gave me the uncanny feeling that he always knew more about everything than he was letting on. I am not the only person he has made this impression on—one of his nephews, Maurice Carr, the son of Singer's sister, wrote of Singer at twenty-two, "He always has such an absent-minded air that at table we expect him to pour a spoonful of soup down his ear-hole. But he is all there. . . ."[2]

As Singer talked to me, I noticed that he looks much kinder than he does in photographs. His small, crumpled face loses its stern expression as he talks, and his light blue eyes water when he laughs. The gentle, cracked tone of his voice and thick accent add to this impression of kindliness. I asked him why he always looks so grim in photographs.

"The camera sees better than you," he replied, smiling. "With people I try to hide whatever is grim or bad, but with the camera I am not so bashful. Anyhow, when the cameraman says, 'Look this way, look that way, look the other way' for three-quarters of an hour, and then he says, 'Be completely natural'—then I look grim!"

During the interview, Singer spoke mostly about his new novel, *Shosha*, which came out while he was teaching at the writers' conference. Like most of his works, the novel is about a world in which the mundane and the supernatural intermingle. The lusts of men and women and the hurly-burly of everyday life in the Jewish ghetto of Warsaw combine with strange coincidences, demons, and curses. And, like most of Singer's works, the novel is deceptively simple, for behind its straightforward narrative lie questions concerning morality, the existence of God, and the struggles between fate and will, will and desire, mind and body.

Although everyday life mingles with the fantastic in all Singer's works, the balance between the two varies. Singer has made *Shosha* one of his more realistic novels, perhaps because it is so autobiographical. The hero, Greidinger, is modeled after Singer in his youth—thin, pale, and red haired; he becomes a vegetarian, as did Singer ("for the sake of the chickens"); his father and younger brothers are rabbis, as were Singer's; and even Shosha herself, the stunted, childlike woman of the novel's title, is based on a girl whom Singer knew in his childhood and has written about in his memoirs. I asked him if the plot of the novel is also autobiograph-ical.

"It is very autobiographical, except that I did not really marry the stunted girl. But I loved her from my childhood. And I met her again, and she was exactly as I write, stunted and small. I am not really ashamed of doing this. There is a saying that all literature is autobiographical. In other words, no matter what you write about, if it didn't happen to you, it might have happened to you."

Singer has been said to be an old-fashioned writer. His stories are not about language or writing. They are not streams of con-sciousness or confessionals. Rather, they are folktale-like yarns about the lives of Jews in pre-Holocaust Poland, about Jewish immigrants in the United States, and about strictly Jewish demons and imps: "I don't have to tell you I'm a Jew," the protagonist says in the story "The Last Demon." "What else, a Gentile? I've heard there are Gentile demons, but I don't know any, nor do I wish to know them. Jacob and Esau don't become in-laws." Singer's stories take place in a magical, foreign world made up partly of history but mostly of his imagination. I asked him if they are based, at all, on folktales he heard as a child.

"Some of them. In most cases not. Like a bird which builds a nest, he would use a little twig, a little straw, a little hay, he doesn't care. The main thing is, the nest should be there. How it is made, how it is glued together, is his own business. The same thing is true in literature. It's whatever can be used to make the story convin-cing, believable, and most of all, interesting."

During the writers' conference, Singer gave four seminars in which he discussed what makes a story interesting. "There should be more events, more facts than thoughts," he said once. "If it's going to be all thinking, you could call it stream of consciousness, but you could also call it stream of boredom. Let me tell you a story. A little boy went to school and said to a friend, 'My father wanted to slap my face today.' He friend said, 'How do you know he wanted to?' The little boy answered, 'Because he did.' The same is true in literature. You know best the thoughts of a person in their actions."

This doctrine was hard for some of Singer's students to accept. "What about experimentation in literature?" they asked. "What about style?" Singer had a ready answer.

"Real experiments in literature are not made by people who worry about style but by nature itself. My experience is that, if a writer really has a story, the story itself creates the style. If he has nothing to say, no style will help."

During his final seminar at the writers' conference, Singer gave his students a special treat by reading a story aloud that he had never published in English, "Sabbath in Gehenna." Sitting at the head of a huge, wooden table, his chin almost resting on the table top, he took off his glasses, cleared his throat, and began.

The story, which takes place in Gehenna (hell), is about how various sinners try to entertain themselves on their one day off from torture a week (the Sabbath). Fires are cooled, torture instruments put away, and the sinners allowed to cavort as they will. One man is musing that he would like to start a magazine and sell it to the angels in Paradise for a profit. "A serious article about atheism in Gehenna would become a smash hit in Paradise," he suggests. His fellow sinners point out that the fires of hell would burn up any magazine well before it reached the newsstands.

Singer read his story slowly, with a clear, varied tone. He paused while the audience laughed, popped one of the cherries a student had brought him into his mouth, and fiddled with his glasses. His hands, holding the manuscript, shook slightly.

After he finished his reading, the fifty or so students in the room broke into applause. Singer put his heavy, black-rimmed glasses back on, smiled, and nodded. But when the noise died down, he said, "Students should criticize their professors, not applaud them."

Four months later, I saw Singer in performance again, only this time he was no longer a mere tutor of fifty or so students, but a celebrity, a Nobel laureate.

I arrived at the B'nai Jeshurun Synagogue on West Eighty-eighth Street in New York three and a half hours before Singer's dialogue with Rabbi Berkowitz was due to begin, for I had been warned that, if I wanted a seat, I'd have to wait that long. For two hours I stood outside the synagogue, watching as people literally fought each other for a place in line. Singer had become a crowd-crushing attraction overnight, inspiring a frenzy that was sometimes violent —a far cry from the indifference with which he was greeted in Berkeley. Once the crowd got inside, the frenzy became even worse, with people shouting at each other and trying to squeeze into every available and sometimes unavailable space. Long after the huge, ornate synagogue was full, people were still pouring in—old women in colorful dresses, men with yarmulkes balanced precariously on their heads, young yeshiva students and teachers. As the crowd grew, tempers shortened.

"Lady, for half the night I've been waiting here. You think this is your seat? If you don't move I'm sitting on you!"

"For twenty years I've belonged to this synagogue—to be treated like this?"

One woman grabbed hold of the back of a pew and swung her hips from side to side, knocking people flying. The noise was so loud people had to shout in each others' ears.

At last, through a small door at the back of the almemar (platform), Rabbi Berkowitz and Singer appeared. Applause filled the room, cameras flashed. Singer stood in the middle of the almemar, bowing and smiling. He looked smaller and more white-faced than ever in the glare of the lights. His smile showed a few gaps in his teeth, and his glasses reflected the flashbulbs. A black velvet yarmulke hid his thin hair almost completely. He went over to the guest table, sat down, took a gulp of water from a glass, and adjusted his microphone. Then he sat still and quiet as he waited for the rabbi to restore order.

The rabbi, a large man with a black beard streaked in gray, took a seat on Singer's left. He looked sternly at the audience over the top of his glasses, like some giant patriarch, and then raised one hand. The crowd quieted. In a slow, dramatic tone he introduced Singer, at unnecessary length. At last he opened the dialogue. "Mr. Singer, or Isaac, as I love to call you. . . ."

During most of the rabbi's verbose questions, Singer behaved respectfully. He listened with attention, the soft folds of his face set in grave lines, and smiled only when the audience laughed at his jokes. But eventually, the pomposity and severity of the rabbi's tone tempted Singer into an irreverent humor I had not seen before. At one point, the rabbi asked Singer for his opinions on marriage.

"I'll tell you, Rabbi," Singer answered, "I don't really like to say these things to a rabbi in a synagogue, but—" and he went on to say that he believes people should divorce after fifteen years of marriage if "they would like to know more about love, more about sex than they know if they live a monogamous life."

The rabbi was greatly displeased with this answer and was stirred to expound with passion and at length on his view of why "the institution called marriage today" is disintegrating. While he was speaking, Singer took off his yarmulke to wipe the sweat from his brow with a handkerchief. He sat bareheaded for a while, listening, and watching the rabbi intently, his yarmulke lying forgotten in his lap. Suddenly, with a pantomime jump, he remembered it and hastily plonked it back on his head. The rabbi ignored this clowning, finished his lecture, and went on to ask Singer how he constructs his working day.

"I'll tell you, Rabbi," Singer said with a visible twinkle, "you speak to me as if I'm a man who makes a program and sticks to it. This is not true. I've broken not only more programs than I have hairs on my head, which I have almost none, but more than you have hairs in your beard." The audience laughed. Rabbi Berkowitz looked severe.

As the dialogue drew to a close, Singer's irreverence surfaced once more. The rabbi had finished his questions and was reading out a long list of future events when about twenty people dropped to their knees, like naughty children trying to keep out of a teacher's sight, and began to creep up to the almemar, all of them holding editions of Singer's books, in the hope of getting an autograph. Singer watched in some alarm as this sea of kneeling people approached, but reached down willingly enough to take the books being waved about at his feet. Just then the rabbi looked up.

"There will be NO signing of books until I have finished my announcements!" he thundered angrily. The autograph hunters retreated and the rabbi resumed his announcements, but Singer continued to sign the books on his lap while the rabbi wasn't looking. Finally, he tossed one toward the audience. It landed on the floor with a resounding slap. The rabbi stopped talking. He did not look up. After a moment's ominous silence, he continued. Until then Singer had managed to keep a straight face, but at this a little grin at last escaped.

Although I had not witnessed this clownish side of Singer before, I had read of it. His nephew, Maurice Carr, has written that Singer "is a superb mime, jester and clown when he chooses," and records a moment at the breakfast table when Singer cracked open a bad egg and said, "Such is life." Carr heard this story from his aunt, Singer's sister-in-law, who recalled, "That's all he said, but how he said it! He has a way with him that is unnatural."[3]

But Singer's naughtiness at the synagogue was not mere buffoonery. It stemmed from a lifetime of rebellion against convention.

Isaac Singer, or Yitzhak Zinger, as his Yiddish name is spelled, was born on July 14, 1904, in a small Polish village. His father was a meek and pious Hasidic rabbi, while his mother was strong-willed, equally pious, but also very down to earth. Her practical view of life clashed with her romantic, dreamy husband's, resulting in a turbulent home life for the whole family.

"My father always used to say that if you don't believe in the *zaddikim* [wonder-rabbis who gave out charms and performed "miracle cures"] today, you won't believe in God," Singer has said. "My mother would say, it's one thing to believe in God and another to believe in a man. My mother's point of view is also my point of view." The clash between Singer's parents forced him to question the religion he was taught, rather than accept it blindly.

When he was four, Singer moved with his parents, older brother and sister, and baby brother, Moishe, from their tiny village to the Jewish ghetto of Warsaw. Singer says the ghetto itself was like a shtetl, or little village, and he has written much about his life there in his memoir *In My Father's Court*. In Warsaw he received the strict education of a rabbi's son, attending first cheder and then yeshiva. His parents wanted him to become a rabbi and expected him to show the appropriate devotion and dedication, but almost as soon as he could read, he began to rebel. He started by asking his father such awkward questions as "Where is God?" "What does He look like?" and "Why do birds fly and worms crawl?"

By the time Singer was ten, he was reading the forbidden secular books that his older brother, Israel Joshua, brought home behind his parents' backs. He read Dostoevsky's *Crime and Punishment* in a Yiddish translation, which affected him profoundly—he was fascinated by the madness and loneliness of Raskolnikov. Other favorite authors were Tolstoy, Chekov, and Strindberg. The reading instilled in Singer both an early curiosity about the world outside his strictly pious household, a world his father considered *tref* (unclean), and an early passion to write.

"At the beginning I tried to imitate other writers. I was in love with Knut Hamsun and tried to imitate him. I read Sherlock Holmes as a boy, a Yiddish translation, and I tried to imitate him in writing and in life. I went into the street and saw a man and said to myself, 'He looks suspicious,' and I followed him. Then he turned around and said, 'Little boy, for what are you following me?' I ran away. That was the end of my career as Sherlock Holmes."

Israel Joshua, who was eleven years older than Singer, was a strong influence on Singer during his childhood and in later life. When Israel Joshua rebelled against his parents, who wanted him also to become a rabbi, and left home to live in an artist's studio, a new world was opened to Singer. He describes a visit to this studio in *In My Father's Court*—the moment he first came face to face with modern secular life.

"After climbing five flights of stairs, I entered a fantastic hall with a large skylight and landscapes, portraits, and nude paintings on the wall. Statues covered with moistened sacks were in the center of the room. I was reminded of a greenhouse which I had once seen, and of a Gentile cemetery. A Hasidic-looking person, small and stooped as a yeshiva boy, happened to be removing one of the sacks, exposing a surprisingly lifelike woman, a kind of female golem who would perhaps shortly perform miracles through the power of the Cabala. Frightened and ashamed, I remained at the door, my mouth open."[4]

By the time he was a teenager, Singer was longing to escape the narrow world of his family. "I found myself stuck in a small village in Poland where my parents had moved," he said. "There was nothing to do or see; I had mud up to my knees even in summer. I dreamed of getting out of there to a city." So he went back to Warsaw on his own to live a harsh life of hunger and poverty, when sometimes he didn't even have a place to sleep, and to pursue his career as a writer.

The decision of Singer and his brother to become writers pained their parents. Their father considered Yiddish novels "sweet poison," and even their mother saw such writings as heretical. They had hoped their sons would write only religious works.

"My father was so ashamed that his children were writing secular works," Singer has said, "that he would tell people we were selling newspapers, an honorable way to make a living. He came to believe this himself. He visited me once and asked me, 'How's the newspaper business going? Are you making a living?' I told him, barely."

Even after escaping the religious lifestyle of his parents, Singer did not stop rejecting traditions or fashions. At that time in Poland, political feelings were running high, and everybody was a socialist, a communist, an anarchist, or a member of one political party or another, but not Singer. He has explained: "My father believed that not only the Ten Commandments were God's commandments, but everything which the rabbis added in two thousand years was also given to Moses on Mount Sinai. The rabbis added all sorts of laws and bylaws, and these were of no use to me. ... Then my brother introduced me to the modern world, and I found that the modern world . . . was making the same kinds of laws and bylaws. So I rebelled against both. I always wanted to be permitted to form my own opinions, to make my own choices as an individual."

This determination to think as an individual led Singer to form his own concept of God, he says, rather than to accept his parents'. He chose to believe in a "higher power," call it God, nature, or merely the Unknown. His thinking was much influenced by the philosophy of Spinoza, whom Singer read with passion for years. Singer likes to explain his belief in God in simple terms.

"If you would come to an island, and you would find there a wristwatch, and someone would tell you that this wristwatch was made by evolution—there was a little metal and a little glass and in the course of a billion years they came together and made a wristwatch—you would say, not even in a billion years. And I say, is the universe less complicated than a wristwatch? So, you must recognize that there is some higher power, some idea, some plan. Once you recognize this, you begin to believe in God."

While Singer was scraping along in Warsaw, he was already breaking conventions by living with a communist woman he now calls only Runia. "We were never married by a rabbi," he has said. "She was my wife. We were very progressive in those days." In 1929, Runia bore him a son, but five years later she went with their son to live in Russia. Singer would not go with her. Later she moved to Israel. Singer didn't see his son again until twenty years later. He has written a story about their uncomfortable reunion, called simply "The Son," which is in the collection *A Friend of Kafka*.[5]

The year after Runia left, Singer lived a lonely life in Warsaw. His brother, by now a famous writer, had gone to live in New York, where he had been offered a job on the Yiddish newspaper the *Jewish Daily Forward;* his parents and younger brother were living in a small village far away; and his sister had moved to England. His few friends were fleeing Poland in fear of Hitler. In 1935, at the age of thirty-one, Singer also fled Poland. He was convinced, wrongly it turned out, that Hitler would invade before the year was out.

Once Singer arrived in New York, with the help of a visa his brother sent him, his life became even lonelier. He could speak no English, had no work and no friends.

"At first New York looked to me most grandiose and at the same time wild, with all these languages, with all these people. I lived then in desolate furnished rooms," he said. "In the beginning I didn't even have a girlfriend. I spent my days wasting time— sitting in cafeterias reading newspapers, taking long walks, talking nonsense like what would you do if you got suddenly a million dollars. I felt that I would never have any roots in this city, or in this country. All these things are not good for writing.

Singer's loneliness in New York, the loss of his family, country, and language, and his dread of the war in Europe that was destroying his people froze his ability to write. He tried one novel, once, but without success.

"I came to this country in 1935, and after two or three years I had the illusion I could write about America," he told me. "I wrote about a man who came from Poland and was disappointed with America. I was disappointed. I have never worked so hard on a novel as this one. There is a wonderful institution in a writer's home—a wastepaper basket. I found I didn't know enough about America. I threw it away, and I felt relief."

For almost seven years he produced no more fiction, living instead on his work as a freelance journalist for the *Forward*. His writing block was further exacerbated by his feelings about Israel Joshua.

"I loved my brother, but I also was somehow ashamed before him that I had failed," Singer said. "I knew that other writers became famous at twenty-five, and here I was already in my thirties and all I had written was one little book in Yiddish which very few people read" (*Satan in Goray*, which he wrote in Warsaw). "I couldn't even make a living. Also, my brother always offered me help which I refused to take. I am not by nature a man who stretches out a hand for help. I don't remember ever having asked a favor from any human being. So, although I adored my brother, I sometimes avoided him so as not to embarrass him or his wife."

Perhaps one of the reasons Singer was lonely for so long was this unwillingness to reach out for help. Even today he is remote from his nephews, Israel Joshua's son, Joseph, and his sister's son, Maurice Carr, and he barely knows their children. Several people who know Singer, but who asked to remain anonymous, told me that he has no close friends but his wife. Carr seems to particularly resent Singer's distance from his kin. He opens his memoir of Singer, *My Uncle Yitzhak*, with the words, "Uncle Yitzhak, if he could help it, would be nobody's uncle, nor brother, nor son, nor husband, nor father, nor grandfather. But in an absurdly ordered world, he is with mock-seriousness all those things."[6]

Although Singer denies that he felt overshadowed by Israel Joshua, only one year after his brother's death in 1945 Singer's writing ability returned. (At this time he also began to attach "Singer" to his previous pen name, Isaac Bashevis, for the first time.) He began then to write short stories and novels at such a prolific rate that his enemies like to say he has written too much and is now only imitating himself. When I asked him if he fears a return of his writer's block, he said, "No, but often I sit down and I don't know what I am going to write. But I do not abandon trying because I have a very old Yiddish typewriter, it is forty-three years old, and I don't want to insult it. So I stay and I try to write.

"But this feeling of literary constipation that people worry about is not a reality. It is a kind of impotence. It's the same thing in sex. If a man goes to bed with a woman, and doesn't immediately feel he is a sexual giant, he shouldn't run out and leave her there. If he has patience, she'll have patience, and sooner or later things will begin to happen. It's the same with writing."

It was many years before Singer was able to support himself solely with his fiction, so he continued to write journalism for the *Forward*, publishing much of it under the name of Warshawsky (the man from Warsaw). Singer signs his full name only to the writing he is proudest of. "For some reason this name is sacred to me," he has said. "Perhaps it's because 'Bashevis' is derived from my mother's name, Bathesheba." Until he won the Nobel prize, Singer was still contributing to the *Forward* and says he will probably continue to do so. He says he likes to be read the same day he writes.

In spite of the abundance of Singer's works, it wasn't until he was fifty-seven years old that he wrote his first potential bestseller, *The Slave*. He has recalled the moment when his editor telephoned with the news.

"He was excited but I was fearful. I will become a bestseller and have no peace. So I prayed to God . . . and asked Him not to give me a bestseller. God listened and said to Himself, 'All these years this poor man has been praying and asking for this and for that. But never have I granted one of his requests. This one I will grant.' " Singer points out that he still has never had a number one bestseller, even now that he has won the Nobel prize.

Singer has by now written eight novels, seven books of short stories, eleven children's books, and three memoirs,* as well as many short stories and essays that have appeared in magazines such as the *New Yorker, Esquire, Harper's,* and *Atlantic Monthly.* His first really popular short story was "Gimpel the Fool," which appeared in a translation by Saul Bellow in 1953. Singer has a joke he likes to tell about it.

"My publisher asked me one day why I thought 'Gimpel the Fool' had been so successful. I said I had an idea. It was because there is in New York a store called Gimbels. People thought of Gimbels the Fool. I said I thought I'd make my next collection Macy the Idiot."

With Singer's first national recognition came bitter criticism from his fellow Yiddish-speaking Jews. Many of them felt, and still feel, that, as the only Yiddish author who is widely read by non-Jews, Singer has a responsibility to depict his culture accurately. And because that culture has been destroyed, and so cannot defend itself, Singer has the further responsibility of being kind about Polish Jews. But Singer's stories of lust, crime, demonology, and the tortures of hell are far from being either historically accurate or kind, a fact that has enraged critics.

One of the main objections these critics make is to the eroticism in Singer's works—the debaucheries of a village claimed by the devil, the restrained lust of a pious rabbi, the overwhelming desires of a bored wife. Even today critics refer to the "pornography" of Singer's fiction. In a 1978 article in the *New York Review of Books,* Leon Wieseltier wrote about the hero of *Shosha:* "His cupidity is insatiable, virtually ideological. And so we are again treated to Singer's stable of randy Jewish women, and again to his customary musings on the spiritual rewards of sex." Later, Wieseltier went on to claim that Singer in fact "detests women" and reduces them to nothing more than that forbidden delight, pork.[7]

Many of the objections to Singer's eroticism, which is actually mild compared to that of many other writers today, have come from the orthodox and the genteel. Not only are they offended by the sexuality itself, but they are outraged that Singer gives it to those who are traditionally meant to be above such things—the pious, the devout, the virginal—in places it is not meant to occur —the bath house, the yeshiva, the rabbinical study. Singer, however, delights in doing just this. "It's just one step from the study

---

* He has written many more books and stories since this writing.

house to sexuality and back again," he has said. "Both phases of human existence have continued to interest me."

The more serious criticism of the sex in Singer's tales is that he gives the impression that pious Jews are riddled with lust and sinfulness, and that he does so in order to sell his stories to a non-Jewish readership. Singer has responded to this criticism often. He did so again at the B'nai Jeshurun Synagogue.

"There is nothing wrong with love and there is nothing wrong with sex," he told the delighted audience. "We are all products of love, and certainly of sex. To say that literature should avoid this most important thing in life is really sheer nonsense. Even the Bible, the Talmud, is full of love and sex stories. They were not afraid of this because they knew it is a part of life. Anyway," he added, playing straight into the critics' hands, "no one is interested in reading a book without love or sex!"

But Singer does not write of sex only to buy readers or because he thinks it is fun (which he undoubtedly does). He dwells on the temptations and delights of the flesh because they are an essential part of his view of humankind. "Singer does not believe we make our own fates or have a free will," a scholar of Yiddish literature and lifelong reader of Singer, Shashka Ehrlich, told me. "His concept of man is one who is ruled by instincts and drives. In all history, in all time, men have been ruled by the same drives. No one can change these, so in a sense the world is timeless." Singer sees fate and desire as analogous, Ehrlich explained, and so his stories about people struggling with lust can be seen as metaphors for the human struggle to control fate.

It is not only the sex in Singer's works that has made critics growl but also the corruption and punishment that sometimes go along with it. One of Singer's earliest and most virulent critics, the highly respected Yiddish poet Jacob Glatstein, has harped at length on this subject. "The author seemingly takes pleasure in the desecration of the dead, which shames the living," he wrote indignantly of Singer's descriptions of the tortures suffered by the souls of sinners. "In these stories, Bashevis bares himself to an extent that makes Yiddish-reading Jews shudder at such naked sadism."[8] Wieseltier, too, objects, calling Singer's literature "a grotesque congeries of the uncanny and the perverse."

Terrible descriptions of hell, where women are hung by their nipples and men burned alive, do, indeed, abound in Singer's stories, but these are not unique to him. They have been a part of Jewish literature for centuries. Singer's older brother illustrated this in his autobiography, *Of a World That Is No More*, when he described their mother's favorite book, *The Rod of Chastisement*.

"The author of this book felt so much at home in Gehenna that he might have been born and raised there. His descriptions of the anguish and the torment inflicted upon the evildoers were fantastic. If a woman merely neglected to shield her bosom while nursing an infant, she ended up with her breasts impaled on glowing hooks. . . . Mother would recite all these cruelties aloud, then douse the pages with scalding tears."[9] In other memoirs and stories, the Singer brothers talk of travelers who came to their childhood home with further such horrible tales of Gehenna.

Singer also incorporates demons into his stories because the fear of the devil and dybbuks (demons that enter and possess a human being) was part of everyday village life among Polish Jews. Yet, the lifelike qualities he gives his supernatural creatures and his literary exaggeration of their frequency of appearance have also incurred criticism. "We are not so superstitious, nor were our people—you are not being accurate!" has been the cry of numerous critics. But Singer's great-niece, Brett (who is also a writer), the granddaughter of Israel Joshua, said to me, "Modern Jews don't like to admit how superstitious their grandparents were," and added that Singer's own father had never seen electricity and didn't even believe in it, although he certainly did believe in dybbuks.

Singer himself claims that he neither intends to indicate that demons and dybbuks really visited Polish Jews all the time nor that they actually exist. Indeed, he is evasive about whether he believes in them at all. He certainly likes to play up his imps and demons—he continually does so in interviews by making his much-loved jokes about some imp who has hidden his glasses or notebook —but when I pressed him on the subject, he was elusive.

"I have never really had any communications with them, and I don't know what they are. If you asked me what is the difference between a hobgoblin and an imp, I wouldn't know. But yes, I have a belief in them. I see them in my daydreams and in my night dreams. I feel that there are powers of which we have no inkling. We haven't yet reached the summit of science, the summit of knowledge."

In the same interview he said, "I always make my stories ambiguous, which means you can explain them from the point of view of the supernatural, or from the point of view of natural psychology. This is my method. It is true that you can explain a dybbuk very easily as a phenomenon of hysteria, and you will be right. You can also explain it as a case of possession. I think that this is the way to do it in our modern times, since people are skeptical. And actually I am myself a skeptic, I would call myself a skeptic with an open mind!"

Whatever Singer's real beliefs, his imps and demons do make excellent metaphorical personifications of human weaknesses. The vanity in one's heart becomes a demon hiding in a mirror. The absentmindedness of old age becomes a mischievous imp playing tricks. The temptation to commit adultery becomes a devil whispering in one's ear. The metaphorical use of the supernatural is a device that has been imbedded in the folklore of many cultures, not just that of Polish Jews.

When Singer talks of his belief in the existence of wonders we do not yet understand, and perhaps never will, he is not so much referring to supernatural phenomena as to his concept of God, that "higher plan" or "idea" he mentioned earlier. I asked Singer in Berkeley if he thinks that a belief in the supernatural, holy or otherwise, is important to one's morality.

"I would say it is very good," he replied. "I will tell you why. Because, if we don't have a belief in the supernatural, we become very haughty. We begin to believe that we have reached the summit of knowledge, and this kind of degenerates people. It takes away the humility which the real sages have, the feeling that we only know a small, small part of what there is to know. And it's especially important for the writer, because if the writer has this kind of illusion that he knows everything, he will prove to the readers that he really knows nothing."

The real objection behind the criticism of Singer's demons and descriptions of hell is that he is painting Jews as sinful, superstitious, and primitive. In other words, that his intention is essentially anti-Semitic—an accusation that has also been leveled at another Jewish writer, Philip Roth. "Bashevis is possibly the first Yiddish writer to put his so-called heroes on the same level with the heroes of non-Jewish literature," wrote the poet Jacob Glatstein. "He dehumanized them, forcing them to commit the most ugly deeds. He brutalized them and made them so obnoxious that the Yiddish reader was repelled by them."[10] All these criticisms boil down to the same question, a question Singer is asked constantly: "Where is your responsibility as a Jewish writer?" Singer's answer rarely varies.

"I am a fiction writer. A fiction writer has a right to invent things —I can invent things which never happened, or which might have happened; no one is going to tell me no. If I wanted to be accurate, I would have become an historian, not a novelist. Actually, that is what fiction is—to get rid of responsibility." In the B'nai Jeshurun Synagogue, he went further, addressing the accusation that he caters to anti-Semitism.

"I do not think I have done any damage to the Jews. Although I describe Jewish thieves and prostitutes, I also describe rabbis and honest men. And if I want to write about a thief, should I write about a Spanish thief or a Chinese thief? Of course I have to write about a Jewish thief. No good reader would think that this means that all Jews are thieves. If a person thinks this way, this means he is already prejudiced. The reader who reads me gets the feeling that here is a writer who is telling the truth, not a writer who tries to prove something which really does not exist. Propaganda and literature are two different things."

Again, this is one of Singer's deceptively simple answers. I am free to write what I want, he says, but the fact remains that what he wants to write is packed with grotesque images, not only of tortures in Gehenna but of deformed and hideous people. I asked him why.

"It is my feeling that life in itself is kind of grotesque," he replied. "And if it isn't grotesque, it is not interesting. If you go deep into human beings, it is grotesque. Let's say when you are with people you behave like any other people. But when you come home, you take off your clothes, you daydream, you are a different kind of person. Things are not as smooth, you may have passions of which you are ashamed, you may have dreams which shock yourself. Since literature goes into the depths of things, it becomes grotesque automatically."

In 1969, Cynthia Ozick wrote a short story that is widely recognized to be based on Singer and his Yiddish critics, which she called, "Envy; or, Yiddish in America." The fictional author in the story, Ostrover, is fairly obviously modeled on Singer.

"He had a moth-mouth as thin and dim as a chalk line, a fence of white hair erect over his ears, a cool voice.

"He was named Pig because of his extraordinarily white skin, like a tissue of pale ham, and also because in the last decade he became unbelievably famous."[11]

Ozick lampoons Singer's stories by describing the plots of Ostrover's tales, but she especially mocks his critics.

"They hated him for the amazing thing that had happened to him—his fame—but this they never referred to. Instead they discussed his style: his Yiddish was impure, his sentences lacked grace and sweep . . . they raged against his subject matter, which was insanely sexual, pornographic, paranoid, freakish. . . ."[12]

The hero of Ozick's story is a failed poet called Edelshtein, who some say is based on Jacob Glatstein. Edelshtein's complaint is that Ostrover only found fame by sleeping with, or buying, the right translators. To succeed in translation is paradoxically seen as a betrayal of tradition and yet as the only way to succeed at all, for there are not enough Yiddish readers to bring fame to any Yiddish writer. Thus Edelshtein simultaneously spits on Ostrover's translators and longs for one himself.

"On account of you I lost everything, my whole life!" Edelshtein shouts down the phone to Ostrover at the end of the story. "On account of you I have no translator!"[13]

Ozick's story is certainly accurate about the problems Yiddish writers have finding translators—a problem particularly acute for writers of a dying language. When Singer first began to write in this country, he had difficulty finding Yiddish readers good enough in English to translate. Now his problem has reversed, and he cannot find translators familiar enough with Yiddish. So, other than his nephew Joseph (the son of Israel Joshua), a painter who has done many of Singer's translations, often uncredited, he uses translators who cannot speak Yiddish at all. His method is to translate his stories himself and then have a writer or editor polish and trim his English.

"My stories would have suffered very much from translation because they are imbued with folklore, and folklore is not easy to translate," Singer said. "But since I do the translation mostly myself, I see to it that my translation does not lose as much as translation as a rule loses. If I see that I have lost something, I try to fill this loss in some way.

"Of course, with translation you can only get an equivalent. Let's say you have an expression in Yiddish, 'Hock mire nischt con chinek,' which, translated, means 'Don't beat the teakettle.' You cannot translate it 'Don't beat the teakettle' because the reader won't know what it means. So you translate it as 'don't talk nonsense, don't boast.' Even though you cannot get the best, you get the next best."

In spite of all these difficulties, Singer insists on continuing to write in Yiddish.

"I feel better when I write in Yiddish," he explained. "The first version of my work is always in Yiddish, where I am home in the language. Also, since I write about people who speak Yiddish, I write in their language. In other words, I don't venture out of my own element. I stay at home with my readers and my heroes. This is good for the story.

"Also, I write in Yiddish so as not to leave my roots. I consider myself a Jewish writer, a Yiddish writer, and I am proud of it. No man lives or creates in a social vacuum, and nativity, religion, and language are more profoundly significant to creative writers than to others. Literature cannot really exist without roots. When you write a love story, the reader wants to know, where did it happen? In San Francisco or New York? It will be different in San Francisco than in New York. It is the same in Tolstoy—somehow a story is not a Moscow story; it's a St. Petersburg story. The greater his roots, the greater a writer's capacity for achievement."

I asked him if he worries that, before long, there will be no one left who can read him in his original Yiddish.

"Yes. The future looks very dark for Yiddish. But, let me tell you, the future of our people looked dark already three thousand years ago. I am not sure that Yiddish will be spoken one hundred years from now, but it will be read, it will be studied in literature, I am sure.

"There is a saying: When you see a Jewish corpse, it doesn't mean that it is going to be a corpse forever. One day it might come back and ask a question."

The last time I saw Singer was on a November evening in New York, the night after his dialogue with Rabbi Berkowitz. He had promised to see me in the hotel suite downtown from his West Side apartment, where he and his wife, Alma, were hiding from the reporters and telephone calls that had been hounding them since Singer's Nobel prize was announced. I had had some difficulty contacting Singer about this interview, for although his telephone number and address are listed for all to see in the Manhattan directory, Alma would not let me speak to him. She knew that Singer had not yet learned to say no to reporters and admirers and was acting as his buffer. However, Singer insisted on keeping his promise, so at last I was allowed my interview.

When I arrived at his hotel room, I heard him and Alma bickering through the door. Her language is German, his Yiddish, so they fight, I discovered, in broken English. I knocked and entered to find him lying on a couch with a coat draped over him, looking exhausted. His small face was paler than ever, except for pink spots on his cheeks, and his wispy hair was mussed up against a pillow. "Please don't ever tell anybody where I am," he asked me, "so people don't call me and I can have some peace." The hotel room was shabby, decorated in dingy greens and browns, and the screech of New York traffic came through the window, but Singer said he didn't mind because it reminded him of Warsaw, "not as big as New York but just as noisy and dirty." To look at his choice of room, one would never guess that Singer is now worth no small amount of money—some say even a million.

Singer asked me to turn on the overhead light and to sit down close to the couch so he could see me. Before we started talking, he put on a pair of dark, green-tinted glasses—his eyes have been troubling him lately—and insisted on testing my tape recorder by reciting a Yiddish poem out loud. Alma came back into the room to listen to the jingling rhyme of the poem, although she understands no Yiddish. She and Singer met in this country and married in 1940. When he finished the poem, Alma announced that she was going to lie down for a while.

"Where will you be, in the bedroom?" Singer asked, craning his neck up to see her from his position on the couch. She nodded, looking apologetic. "Oh," he said with a laugh, "go lie down!" Although younger than he, Alma also looked tired and harrassed. When she had left, we spoke about the night at the synagogue.

"I had the greatest difficulty entering the place last night," he said. "I had to smuggle myself in, else they would have torn me to pieces!"

I asked him what he thought of the rabbi's questions about his critics, the same questions they all ask him—why do you write this dirty stuff? Aren't you responsible to your fellow Jews? Singer waved impatiently.

"I don't bother with these critics. I don't even read them. If I get a newspaper or a magazine, and I by accident see an article about me, I will look into it. But really, I believe that a writer should be completely free of these things, and be only responsible to the muse, if there is a muse, and to nobody else."

"But," I objected, "I read an article of yours called, 'Yiddish, a Language of Exile' in which you said that you felt a responsibility to keep the Yiddish language alive through your writing."

"I said that? From this you can see how little responsible I am," Singer said with a laugh. "One day I give one answer, another day I give another answer. Actually, all motivations are not concise. Motivation depends on mood, on the moment.

"I write first of all because I want to write. The second thing is that it is easier for me to write in Yiddish. I never really sit down to write because I want Yiddish to keep up existing. If I like I can say so, but I tell you it's not true. No writer sits down with this kind of motivation. It's the same thing if you would say that you marry because you want that the human race should continue to exist. It's not true. You want to have a baby with a man because you love the man, not because you love humanity."

"But," I said again, recalling the interview in which Singer had said it was "a tragedy and a responsibility to be one of the last Yiddish writers," "don't you feel a responsibility to keep up the traditions of Yiddish literature?" Singer shrugged and looked slightly defiant.

"You heard what I said at the synagogue? I don't care about the traditions of Jewish literature. Let them have their tradition, I am going to create my own. That is all I care about. I feel free, like a bird."

Now that Singer is a Nobel laureate, he has little to worry about as far as his responsibility toward the Yiddish language is concerned. Yiddish has always been considered a "jargon" or "spoiled German," a kitchen language of curses and ignorant sentiments. Now, even Singer's critics are pleased that he has brought Yiddish to the attention of the world as a language in its own right, capable of beauty and elegance. Singer knows this, too. He spoke of it to the synagogue audience.

"When I got the cable [announcing the prize], I answered that the Yiddish readers feel that the prize was also given to them and to Yiddish. They are justified to feel so."

Singer is pleased about the prize, for the sake of Yiddish as well as for himself, but he is less pleased at the consequences of his new fame.

"Since I got the Nobel prize, people are recognizing me in the street. It never happened to me before, except sometimes on the West Side, where I live. But I will tell you the truth. I like really not to be recognized in the street. I like to have the feeling that when I walk in the street, I know the street but the street doesn't know me." I asked him if he thinks having won the prize will make him feel that he no longer needs to write, that he has achieved all he can.

"No, I feel that as long as I live, I want to do my work. As a matter of fact, I haven't worked much for the past four weeks and I feel already that I miss my work so much that I'm just looking forward to the moment when I will be able to sit down and do it. I'm ready to do a lot of things for people, but not to let them take away my time of work." He paused and sat in silence for a while, gazing at an empty ashtray on the coffee table. "The Nobel prize has not changed me," he went on. "I am still the same Isaac Singer. My thinking and emotions are still the same." He pushed the coat off his lap and hoisted himself up a bit on the couch.

"I remember when I was a child, although it happened almost seventy years ago, I went out and played with a few little boys. They were sitting under a broken umbrella, and I wanted also to sit under the umbrella, but they didn't let me in. So I said, 'You must let me in, I have new shoes.' And immediately the children decided, if he has new shoes, he has to sit under the broken umbrella.

"I think that grown-up people also behave this way—if he has got the prize, he has become more important. Actually, I am grateful for the prize, but no prize changes a man. If a man is changed by a prize, he is not worth a prize."

SINGER COMMENTARY

I wrote this profile of Isaac Bashevis Singer twelve years ago, and Singer has continued to produce novels, memoirs, and stories ever since. As he promised, the Nobel prize did not change him.

I remember first coming across Singer's stories in the *New Yorker* when I was an undergraduate in England and assuming that the author was long since dead, since the stories had such a peculiar, Old World feeling to them. I believe that before he won the prize, a lot of other people also thought of him as dead, or at least as a writer of the past. I was understandably excited, therefore, when I discovered that not only was Singer very much alive but that he was coming to teach at Berkeley. I decided then to interview him and found him easily approachable, if somewhat vague.

"I had the impression there were people coming to see me today," he said in his room at one point, "but it seems they are all coming tomorrow. I make mistakes. I never write things down. I do such things that I am astonished. I make two appointments at the same time with two different people, and then I have to apologize. I was sitting here, not knowing for sure if it's today or Friday; meanwhile you came in, so I had a chance to talk to you."

He granted me two interviews in his room and permission to use material from his seminars, which I attended for free. Singer knew I had no publisher at the time of the interviews but did not seem to mind, especially once I had proved myself serious by getting hold of an early copy of *Shosha* from the publisher, reading it, and interviewing him about it before it had even reached the stores. ("You mean to say you read the whole book from the beginning to the end?" he said in astonishment. "When did this happen, yesterday?") I also followed him to various conferences and book parties, taking the opportunity to watch him in different settings.

I wrote a question-and-answer article based on those first interviews that was published by the *San Francisco Review of Books* in September 1978 under the title "Demons, Goblins, and Autobiography." I sent the piece to Singer in New York; he liked it, which helped gain me access to him later on. But I was not satisfied. I wanted to write more about him, to get to know him better. I decided to write my master's thesis on him (I was a graduate student in journalism at Berkeley at the time), so I telephoned him in New York and extracted a promise from him to let me interview him again for a longer piece. Little did I know how important that promise was to prove.

For the next few weeks I immersed myself in Singer stories and interviews, until Yiddish phrasing was dancing in my dreams. I also discovered through a friend that Singer's great-niece Brett Singer—now a published novelist—was in graduate school at Stanford. I met and interviewed her, and although she was constrained to be tactful about her turbulent family, she was a great help in suggesting other sources and readings. Meanwhile, I sent off query letters and called around, trying to get an assignment for the piece.

Then Singer won the Nobel prize. As soon as I heard the news, I called his secretary in New York, who knew me from my previous article, and she gave me Singer's number in Florida. I phoned him and tried to arrange a time when I could come to New York, but he was harassed and would not commit himself. He did tell me he would be in New York in November, however, so I resolved to go on the off-chance that he would make time to see me, expense be hanged. Meanwhile, I published a second article about him, "Conversations with Isaac Singer," a personal account of my meeting with him, in *California Living*, the Sunday magazine of the *San Francisco Examiner*.

In November I flew to New York with a list of contacts—Singer's friends, translators, editors—which I had obtained from books, Brett, and magazine articles. If I didn't get to see him, I decided, at least I wouldn't have wasted the trip.

At first I couldn't get through to Singer in New York, for his wife would never let me speak to him. They were both fed up with publicity. So I spent my days (I had only a week) interviewing Yiddishists and translators. I remember making an appointment with Singer's editor at the *Jewish Daily Forward*. I rode the long distance down Fifth Avenue in a bus and, being unused to New York and the diesel fumes, became so carsick that I had to get off the bus halfway. By this time I was late; so I fought down my nausea and called the editor to apologize and cancel our appointment. He was disgusted with me.

Finally I heard about the dialogue with Rabbi Berkowitz, which was free and open to the public. After the interminable wait and some battling with the astonishingly aggressive crowd, I managed to tape record the dialogue and to take some photographs of Singer. Meanwhile, I kept telephoning him, thinking that I might have to go to his door and knock on it, uninvited, if worse came to worst.

At last Singer consented to speak to me. He was impressed that I had flown all the way to New York to see him, and felt guilty enough about his earlier promise to give in. He was apologetic and kind about having put me off for so long and gave me the address of his secret hideout. That last interview was more casual and relaxed than the previous ones, partly because I was less in awe of Singer and partly because he was too exhausted to be on guard. After asking me a long string of questions about me and my family genealogy, trying to dig up every ounce of Jewishness I had in my roots, he looked at me curiously and said, "What made you decide to write a thesis about me?" And at the end of the interview, as I was checking over my notes for last questions, he said something that is music to any biographer's ears.

"I think you know about me more than I know myself!"

I went back to Berkeley and wrote several versions of the profile, selling them to different markets. As well as the two pieces mentioned earlier, I published a profile of Singer in *Writer's Digest* in May 1980, entitled "Never Insult a Yiddish Typewriter," and another in a children's magazine called *New Wings*, which is now defunct. The lesson in this is that even though the piece included here, which was the most comprehensive, was too long for magazines, I could compartmentalize and sell four different versions of it. By using different material, varying the forms, and going to separate markets that did not overlap, I managed to do this without infringing on anyone's copyright.

The biggest challenge in writing this piece was organizing it. Everything Singer said was so quotable that my piece kept growing and growing, even when I tried to cut out the anecdotes I found he repeated to every reporter. Finally I read through all my transcripts and notes, made a list of the major subjects (Singer's childhood, Singer's marriage, Singer's critics, etc.), and color-coded them: black was biography, blue was critics, red was Singer on literature, green was demonology, and so on. I organized the subjects into a basic outline for the profile, then went through all the transcripts again, color-coding the quotations to match the subjects.

The next stage was to write out the piece in rough, putting the quotations in order. At that point I had to get ruthless and sacrifice a lot of good material to avoid repetition. Lastly, I wrote out draft upon draft of the piece.

I took a break of five weeks, hysterical from rewriting. I had become so immersed in the piece that I couldn't see it, and just the thought of it made me want to weep. Back after the break, I was able to make considerable changes in the organization. I was helped by the patient editing of Bernard Taper, one of my professors at Berkeley.

I never grew bored with Singer as a subject, however tired of my own writing I became, because he was so complex and intriguing. Each time I saw him brought a new revelation—an experience I tried to describe to the reader in my opening section. Singer evolved from a charming, absentminded old man to a wily, brilliant rebel.

His irreverence in the synagogue, his impatience in the hotel room afterward, and above all the cleverness of his writing showed me how often he had pulled the wool over journalists' eyes. Since my piece at least two full-length biographies of him have been published, but at the time I had only literary critics and other journalists to guide me. I wanted to break through Singer's act and reach to something deeper.

I attempted to achieve this depth by writing little essays to myself, labeled "The Private Singer," "Singer on Writing," and so on. In other words, I had to break away from facts and go to interpretation. Here is some of what I wrote.

"The overwhelming feeling I got when I first met Singer was that he was irresistably charming in a wise, dignified, sagelike way. I felt tremendous respect for his whitened hair and little crumpled face that looks ten years older than it is. I felt wonder at the wit and wisdom that came out at his every phrase, wit that betrayed a certain indifference and irreverence toward convention; wisdom that held some sadness and bitterness and a sense of long experience with the harsher side of life. But my overall impression was of optimism, and that Singer has a great respect for his fellow men and women.

"As he became more familiar to me, both through reading hundreds of interviews with him and through listening and talking to him, my awe lessened. I never lost the feeling that he was generous and deeply polite, that he cannot say no to a request, but I began to see that his wit was practiced and polished and that his irreverence contained some contempt. Also, I saw that part of his wit consisted in twisting questions around to suit the answers he had already found success with in the past. He was a tricky customer. No one, to my belief, has ever got the truth out of him about whether and how he believes in God, what he really thinks about Jews, or about his personal life; his feelings about his first wife and older brother, for instance. Also, as well as the dignity and sagacity that had first impressed me, there was a streak of real naughtiness. And a little impatience, especially with pomposity and overt flattery. I ended up thinking of him as being a little devilish, very private, something of an actor, yet utterly brilliant."

Most of these thoughts got into my piece, although not all. I had a journalistic obligation to be fair, to try to compare my insights to those of others before I foisted them on the world. So I selected the most proven of my theories, used first person to cover myself, and left out the rest. The result is a piece that is as much an essay on Singer as a profile; a piece that aptly illustrates Susan Sontag's description of the literary profile as whatever the writer wants it to be.

Being on the Receiving End

■

by Jessica Mitford

A book on profiles and interviewing would not be complete without hearing from the other side.

The absolutely worst sort of interview is when a reporter telephones in order to do a round-up of local opinion on something or other, and you are supposed to give an off-the-cuff snappy answer: "Where were you when Kennedy was assassinated?" "Where were you when the first men landed on the moon?" "What's the best book you have read this year?" A columnist from the *San Francisco Chronicle* phoned my husband with just such a request: "What's your idea of hell?" Bob, not skipping a beat, replied, "Being interviewed by you."

Next worst is the interview that starts out, "I haven't read any of your books, but I'd like to do a profile of you for XYZ magazine."

There was just such a moment (memorable, as it was way back in 1963) when I was doing a book tour publicizing *The American Way of Death.* I think this was in Tulsa, Oklahoma. I arrived at an early morning television show; the act preceding mine was a group of little kids doing push-ups, cheered on by devoted moms. The blonde, beehived hostess announces: "And our next guest is Miss Jessie Medford. Please give her a hand." I get up on the stage. Hostess whispers: "What have you done?" Me: "Wrote a book." Hostess: "Miss Medford has written a lovely novel, and she's going to tell us all about it."

Adversary interviews can be enjoyable, however. After my book on prisons, *Kind and Usual Punishment,* came out, I was invited to be on William Buckley's "Firing Line." The setup was a TV studio in San Francisco, with a live audience. I put out the word, and filled the audience with all the ugly mugs from the Prisoners Union, an ex-convict group, plus students whom I had taught at San Jose State University—and to top it all, my son Benjy with his huge dog Jekyll. I had studied Buckley's technique—mostly, "When did you stop beating your wife?"—and thanks to spirited and inspiring audience response, didn't get too badly dented. Modesty should (but doesn't) prevent me from concurring with the audience that I won the debate.

Best of all, once in a great while along comes an interviewer who has taken the trouble to read one's work—and to avoid stock questions that inevitably lead to trite canned answers. Just the other day I had the pleasurable experience of a visit from two twelve-year-olds, Lill Weir and Cristina Martin, who wanted an interview for their self-published magazine. Aside from being immensely gratified (as any writer would be) that my books should have attracted the attention of these very young readers, I was struck by the originality of their whole approach, in which they managed to drag me back in time over six decades to a girl their age.

At the other end of the scale—that is, the adult-professional end—was the unforgettable arrival at our house of Helen Benedict. Somehow, she seemed to have got the point of everything straight away, beginning with Bob's victorious lawsuit. In her introduction, Benedict says that "During an interview, the reporter is a receiver." That wasn't at all my impression of our discussion; I seem to remember lots of mutual chatting and giggling away at various things, the three of us having a good time reminiscing. Perhaps that is her secret weapon as an interviewer; and perhaps one day Lill and Cristina, who are themselves good gigglers/chatters, will glean further insight into the mysterious craft of interviewing from this amusing and instructive book.

NOTES

PREFACE

1. Ira Bruce Nadel, *Biography: Fiction, Fact, and Form* (London: Macmillan, 1984), p. 10. Nadel cites Karl Popper, *Conjectures and Refutations: The Growth of Scientific Knowledge*, 2d ed. (New York: Basic Books, 1965), p. 46.

INTRODUCTION

1. Leon Edel, *Writing Lives: Principia Biographica* (New York: Norton, 1984), p. 14.
2. Tom Wolfe and E. W. Johnson, *The New Journalism* (New York: Harper and Row, 1973), pp. 51–52.
3. Samuel Johnson cited in Jeffrey Meyers, ed., *The Craft of Literary Biography* (London: Macmillan, 1985), p. 1.
4. Wolfe, *The New Journalism*, p. 219.
5. John Hersey, *Life Sketches* (New York: Knopf, 1989), p. 254.
6. Wolfe, *The New Journalism*, p. 331.
7. Hunter S. Thompson, *The Hell's Angels* (New York: Ballentine, 1966).
8. Frances Fitzgerald, *Cities on a Hill* (New York: Simon and Schuster, 1981), p. 247.
9. Jane Kramer, *The Last Cowboy* (New York: Harper and Row, 1978).
10. T. S. Eliot quoted in Edel, *Writing Lives*, pp. 21–22.
11. Joan Didion, *The White Album* (New York: Washington Square Press, 1979), p. 79.
12. Hersey, *New Yorker*, July 28, 1945.

13. John McPhee, *The John McPhee Reader* (New York: Vintage Books, 1978), p. 408.
14. Hersey, *Life Sketches*, p. 143.
15. Didion, *The White Album*, pp. 21–25.
16. Joan Didion, "Mrs. Reagan's White House," *New York Review of Books*, December 21, 1989.
17. John Gregory Dunne, *Harp* (New York: Simon and Schuster, 1989), p. 79.
18. Edel, *Writing Lives*, p. 15.
19. Woolf quoted in Nadel, *Biography: Fiction, Fact, and Form*, p. 5.
20. Pachter, ed., *Telling Lives* (Washington, D.C.: New Republic Books, 1979), p. 64.
21. I owe a debt to James Thurber for this.

2. Flight from Predictability: Joseph Brodsky

1. Joseph Brodsky, "Plato Elaborated," in *A Part of Speech* (New York: Farrar, Straus, and Giroux, 1977), p. 131.
2. Brodsky, "Ecologue IV: Winter," *New Yorker*, March 29, 1982, pp. 46–47.
3. Brodsky, "New Stanzas to Augusta," in *Selected Poems* (New York: Harper and Row, 1973), pp. 57–59.
4. Brodsky, "To a Certain Poetess," *ibid.*, p. 104.
5. Brodsky, "Eimen alten Architekten in Rom," *ibid.*, p. 119.
6. Brodsky, "A Part of Speech," in *A Part of Speech*, p. 93.
7. Brodsky, "1972," *ibid.*, p. 65.
8. Brodsky, "Lagoon," *ibid.*, p. 74.
9. Brodsky, "The Classical Ballet," *ibid.*, p. 77.

4. Filling Silences with Strong Voices: Paule Marshall

1. Leon Edel, *Writing Lives* (New York: Norton, 1984), p. 15.

5. Morals and Surprises: Bernard Malamud

1. From Malamud's first-person entry in *World Authors*, 1975. Cited in *Current Biography* (New York: H. H. Wilson, 1978), p. 274.
2. Bernard Malamud, *God's Grace* (New York: Avon, 1982), pp. 156–57.
3. Ralph Tyler, "A Talk with the Novelist," *New York Times Book Review*, February 18, 1979, p. 1.
4. Review of *The Tenants* by Morris Dickstein, *New York Times Book Review*, October 3, 1971, p. 1.

5. Israel Shenker, *New York Times Book Review,* October 3, 1971, p. 20.
6. Dickstein, Review of *The Tenants.*
7. Katha Pollit, "Bernard Malamud," *Saturday Review,* February 1981, p. 34.

6. INTREPID TWOSOME: JESSICA MITFORD AND ROBERT TREUHAFT

1. Jessica Mitford, *A Fine Old Conflict* (London: Michael Joseph, 1977), p. 102.
2. Jessica Mitford, *Daughters and Rebels* (New York: Avon Books, 1960), pp. 29–30.
3. Mitford, *A Fine Old Conflict,* p. 33.
4. *Ibid.,* p. 36.
5. *Ibid.,* p. 108.
6. Tom Wolfe, *The New Journalism,* p. 51.

9. NEVER INSULT A YIDDISH TYPEWRITER: ISAAC BASHEVIS SINGER

1. Isaac Bashevis Singer, "Yiddish, The Language of Exile," *Judaica Book News* (1976), 6 (2):23.
2. Maurice Carr, "My Uncle Yitzhak," *Congress Monthly,* November 11, p. 11.
3. *Ibid.*
4. Isaac Bashevis Singer, *In My Father's House* (New York: Signet Books, 1967), pp. 173–74.
5. Isaac Bashevis Singer, *A Friend of Kafka* (New York: Farrar, Straus, and Giroux, 1970).
6. Maurice Carr, "My Uncle Yitzhak."
7. Leon Wieseltier, "The Revenge of Isaac Bashevis Singer," *New York Review of Books,* December 7, 1978, p. 6.
8. Jacob Glatstein, "The Fame of Isaac Bashevis Singer," *Congress Bi-Weekly,* March 7, 1966, p. 17.
9. Israel Joshua Singer, *Of a World That Is No More* (New York: Vanguard Press, 1970).
10. Glatstein, "The Fame of Singer."
11. Cynthia Ozick, "Envy; or, Yiddish in America," in *The Pagan Rabbi and Other Stories* (New York: Shocken Books, 1976), p. 46.
12. *Ibid.,* p. 47.
13. *Ibid.,* p. 100.

INDEX